How To Develop And Manage Successful Distributor Channels In World Markets

How To Develop And Manage Successful Distributor Channels In World Markets

William C. Fath

amacom
American Management Association
New York • Atlanta • Boston • Chicago • Kansas City • San Francisco • Washington, D.C.
Brussels • Mexico City • Tokyo • Toronto

This book is available at a special
discount when ordered in bulk quantities.
For information, contact Special Sales Department,
AMACOM, a division of American Management Association,
135 West 50th Street, New York, NY 10020

This publication is designed to provide accurate and authoritative
information in regard to the subject matter covered. It is sold with
the understanding that the publisher is not engaged in rendering
legal, accounting, or other professional service. If legal advice or
other expert assistance is required, the services of a competent
professional person should be sought.

Library of Congress Cataloging-in-Publication Data

Fath, William C.
    How to develop and manage successful distributor channels in world
markets / William C. Fath.
        p.   cm.
    Includes index.
    ISBN 0-8144-0306-9
    1. Export marketing.   2. Distributors (Commerce)   3. Marketing
channels.   I. Title.
HF 1416.F38   1995
658.8'48—dc20   95-38024
                                                           CIP

Printing number

10   9   8   7   6   5   4   3   2   1

This book is dedicated to the distributors around the world who have shared their entrepreneurial business sense with me and served as my mentors.

Contents

Acknowledgments

To paraphrase the adage, "No man is an island and no author can stand alone."

My many thanks to the staff of AMACOM, especially Mary Glenn, acquisitions editor; Richard Gatjens, associate editor; Kate Pferdner, managing editor; and my developmental editor, who never seemed to tire of me, Jacqueline Flynn.

I also want to thank Michael Coleman of Baker & McKenzie, who has for many years provided me with excellent materials regarding the legal aspects of dealing with distributors in other countries.

Last, but not least, I wish to thank those who have attended my American Management Association and other seminars for their insights, sharing of their business experiences, and their encouragement to "write a book".

How To Develop And Manage Successful Distributor Channels In World Markets

Introduction

Approximately 35 percent of the industrial goods gross domestic product (GDP) and 27 percent of the consumer goods GDP of the United States are sold through distributors. In the total world market the sales of goods through distributors is estimated to be approximately 40 percent, according to the U.S. Department of Commerce, and this figure is increasing (estimated to be 47 percent by 2000) as more and more companies enter the world market.

The independent distributor, therefore, must be considered a key player in international commerce and should be an integral component of any company's sales and marketing strategy.

The independent distributor can add value for the end user in terms of one-stop shopping, just-in-time delivery programs, electronic data interchange, contract purchasing, and total supply contracts. Very few of the distributor's suppliers are able to offer these same value-added services to the end-user customer. There are very few companies that have the resources to identify and understand the myriad of world markets, their diverse cultures and their particular buying habits. A properly selected distributor knows the market and its buying habits, and is an integral part of the local culture. The distributor knows local law and finance, political considerations, and the customers to whom you desire to sell. This knowledge is invaluable when you consider that the cost of supporting a direct salesperson to "learn the territory" in today's market could easily exceed $300,000.

This book will assist you in selecting and managing distributors as a primary sales channel in key world markets. It shows you how to use time-tested management strategies and tactics and makes you aware of some of the cultural diversities and legal considerations you are likely to experience in selecting, working with, and managing a distributor sales network.

By definition, the distributor is one who "takes title" to your goods for their own account for resale. Legally, the term *distributor* seldom appears in law journals or the written laws of countries. Instead, *reseller* is the word most frequently used. If your distributor does not purchase your goods but merely sells them on your behalf, then the seller is legally considered an *agent*. It is important to make this distinction at the outset, as many companies that are actually agents refer to themselves as distributors.

There is no such thing as a " nonstocking distributor." This distinction is important under most country laws. Distributors who buy for their own account seldom can claim severance upon termination of a sales agreement. However, agents are protected under most countries' laws and can claim severance upon termination, especially if they have been authorized to act on the supplier's behalf in signing certain legal documents or making certain financial commitments.

Some of you deal through "systems integrators," "value-added resellers," and other titles of convenience; however, if the people who resell your product actually purchase the product from you for their own accounts, then they have "taken title" and are considered resellers, thereby coming under the same legal category as distributors.

Reasons for Using the Independent Distributor Channel

Cultural Considerations

Distributors know how the market buys, how major customers make buying decisions, and what the hierarchy of decision makers is in those accounts to whom you desire to sell. A good distributor knows how to position and sell your products within the local market culture, will provide product availability, and will enhance your company's identity in the desired market.

If properly selected, distributors will cooperate in strategic market planning and tactical sales planning. They know their markets and how your products should be promoted and sold.

Political Considerations

Good distributors know local law and are most likely aware of import and tariff restrictions on your products. They will have local knowledge of customs administration and processing.

In developing markets or economies, many distributors can reduce the costs of imports by showing that your products enhance the local economy by providing jobs and/or revenue enhancement. Wherever possible, you should be aware of the impact of your products on the local economy and publicize your contribution. This is especially true in India, North Africa, and the Philippines.

Economic Considerations

Distributors provide product availability and inventory financing in the desired market. The costs of inventory possession are a negative on a company's cash flow. Because distributors maintain this inventory, these costs of possession are borne by the distributors.

Distributors reduce your selling costs by providing local credit and collection, value-added manufacturing or customization, packaging your products with complementary or supplementary products, local promotion, and advertising and reduced costs of product introduction. Each of the above services offered by distributors has a measurable dollar value and a positive impact on your cash flow. Therefore, distributor's discounts are not given, they are earned!

How the Distributor Channel Can Work for You

In this book, you will learn how to identify world markets and the distributors who serve these markets, how to interview and select the right distributors for your products, and how to gain and maintain the loyalty of the selected distributors.

You will further learn what payment, pricing, and discount strategies you should be prepared to implement as well as some of the legal ramifications you will face in certain markets.

The book contains a number of forms that will help you in these processes, and blank forms are presented in Appendix C that you can fill out yourself.

To be successful in world markets, you must be prepared to implement multilevel marketing strategies and use different strategies for each market. Too many companies still believe in the "one strategy fits all" theory of marketing; it will never be so!

A company that enters the world arena must take as its tenet the following six words:

Markets Dictate Strategy
Strategy Dictates Organization

Politicians preach local market protection, aid to local or national markets, balanced trade instead of free trade, and sanctions against those who,"Don't do it our way. However, if they want to compete globally, companies cannot afford to think in these narrow terms. Companies that believe that there is an industry standard of doing business, or that "my country's method of business conduct must prevail," are going to be very disappointed in the world marketplace.

Even though it is now past history and was uttered before the phrase "market economy" became accepted by most of the world, the following advice came from a gentleman who never ran a business nor belonged to the corporate world:

Today it is hardly possible to preserve any sort of closed society. The world economy is becoming a single organism, outside of which, not a single state can develop normally, whatever social system it belongs to or whatever economic level it has reached.

The speaker was Mikhail Gorbachev at the United Nations, 1988. His statement epitomizes global thinking and should be incorporated into your global marketing strategies.

Chapter 1

Identifying Your World Markets

To many of us, the world market is a vast gray area of different cultures, languages, styles, habits, laws, accepted practices, business customs, and many other differences atypical to our normal way of doing business—that is, normal in our terms and in the terms of the United States and its business standards. In the marketplace, our frame of reference is usually business practices we have learned and become accustomed to in our own country.

When we enter world markets, our normal business practices may suddenly become unacceptable or illegal, and we may find ourselves questioning the business morality or practices of others.

In many countries, the simple matter of a credit request or a request for a credit reference can be an insult. A payment for services rendered to gain an introduction or access to a new market may be considered a bribe. An exclusive agreement may be illegal. A noncompetitive clause in a sales agreement may carry with it a prohibition forbidding you, as the supplier, from consummating any direct sales in the distributor's assigned market area. A time-worn logo could be misinterpreted and/or convey a message different from that which was originally intended.

The stories concerning misinterpreted logos are legion. Words like *bummer*, used in a Burger King commercial, and the reference to V8 juice's giving one "spunk" both have slang sexual connotations in England. The Spaulding Company offered the Japanese four golf balls for the price of three as a promotion; but in Japan, 4 is considered an unlucky number, like 13 in the United States—and we all know how superstitious golfers can be. The words "marked down" mean literally the direction down in Brazil, so if a product is "marked down" it is destined for hell. Your corporate strategy that worked so well for you in the United States and Europe may die in Brazil or elsewhere, owing to vernacular and slang connotations of translated words.

Your well-paid "foreign" agents, brokers, or newly appointed distributors may be disciples of misinformation. They will tell you only what they want you to know about their markets and/or customers for fear that you will "steal" their customers, discuss a price that they may have artificially inflated, or learn that they are diverting products to other markets, counterfeiting your goods, or worse. So how are you to know whom to trust and support with the name and image of your company?

For all of these reasons, and more, the process of identifying and learning about your new markets, the cultures of those markets, and the best distributors therein is critical and should not be treated lightly. The distributor selection process is time-consuming and difficult, but the costs of a bad decision in selecting distributors can far outweigh the expense and time it takes to select one properly in the first place.

The responsibility for identifying markets is yours. The primary concern of distributors, agents, brokers, and the like is the sale of products and not market research. You cannot delegate the responsibility for market research and/or identification of potential customers to your distributors; however, your distributors may be excellent sources of information and may be extremely cooperative in "jointly" developing marketing plans. Before you can expect this level of cooperation, however, you must be able to demonstrate your knowledge of the distributors' markets and have a sales plan in place to sell to the distributors' existing accounts and to expand each distributor's account base.

Current Account and Market Profile

The Target Market Profile is a spreadsheet that can be easily prepared on paper or as a precalculated computer spreadsheet. It is basically an extrapolation of your current business that defines those vertical markets in which you have had past sales success. The Target Market Profile is merely what it says, a profile, and should not be confused with any form of forecasting or a substitute for basic market research. (See Exhibit 1-1, Target Market Profile.)

Customer List

Begin your market identification with a review of your current customer list. Identify those customers who, combined, represent 80 percent of your sales revenue. Enter the names of these customers in column 1. Classify these customers by their industry or business. Many governments use the Standard Industrial Classification (SIC) codes developed in the United States to identify a company's core business. Enter the SIC, or the description of the customers industry, in column 2.

In column 3, enter your annual sales to each customer.

Size Factor

Your size factor, which predicts customers' purchasing power or their ability to purchase from you, goes in column 4. To select a size factor, find a customer statistic, such as the number of employees or square footage of floor space allocated to your products, that correlates as nearly as possible with your sales volume to that customer.

For instance, if you believe that a customer's ability to purchase is proportional to his profitability, and that profitability is proportional to productivity, then "number of employees" may be a valid size factor. Other options might be shelf space allocated for your products, the customer's sales revenues, the customer's power use, the customer's unit production volume, or the consumer population in the customer's town or region.

Chart your sales to each customer during a specific period of time. Then create charts for the statistics you are considering

Exhibit 1-1. Target Market Profile.

CUSTOMER LIST

(1) Customer Name	(2) Industry SIC Code	(3) Annual Sales To ($000)	(4) Size Factor (#EMP)	(5) Sales/Emp. ($)
J&L	3522	450	800	563
METRO	2819	360	750	480
LANDFALL	2221	341	650	525
KLINKER	3632	340	800	425
FABCOM	3632	328	600	547
AJAX	2259	310	370	838
CONTINENTAL	3535	260	400	650
PIERCE	3522	235	500	470
NACOM	2874	180	250	720
SMITH & SONS	2259	162	320	506
EASY-GLO	2874	135	180	750
GENERAL WIDGET	3535	122	200	610
CONSOLIDATED	2259	120	160	750
BROWN & JONES	2819	111	180	617
ZENIX	2819	110	210	524
WORLDWIDE	3535	97	100	970
QUANTUM	3535	89	150	593
BAKER	2221	85	200	425
DICEY	3522	60	410	146
TOTAL		3,895		

INDUSTRY LIST

(6) Industry SIC Code	(7) Sales/Emp. ($)	(8) Total Employment	(9) Est Sales Poten. ($000)
3522	436	44,000	19,184
3632	448	56,000	25,088
2259	696	65,000	45,240
2819	764	38,000	29,032
3535	668	81,000	54,108
2221	501	92,000	46,092
2874	733	67,000	49,111
			267,855

as a size factor for those same customers. Select the statistic whose graph most closely correlates with your sales chart as your size factor.

Once you have a size factor, you can use the sales-per-size factor ratio to gauge the actual sales to a particular customer against his potential sales. Calculate the sales-per-size factor ratio for the entire industry, then compare that number to the sales-per-size factor ratio for the particular customer. If the ratio for an entire industry is $400 per employee, but your ratio with that customer in that industry is only $300, you can estimate that you have the potential to increase sales to that customer by 33 percent.

If you find no size factors that work as good predictors of your sales with specific customers, then use an overall market indicator. Buying power indices and industrial purchasing power indices are published annually by the Bureau of Labor Statistics and in *Sales & Marketing Management* magazine. Other economic indicators are published weekly in *Business Week*, the *Wall Street Journal*, the Sunday *New York Times*, the *Economist*, and the *Financial Times*. Each publication with these indicators has between twenty-five and ninety entries, depending on the publication. Whichever size factor you select, it should be information that is readily available.

To choose your size factor from all the economic statistics available, chart your sales volume over the past three years and compare it with the published list of leading economic indicators during those years. Select those indicators that closely parallel your sales performance. You will most likely find three to five indicators that parallel your past sales performance.

Then, to calculate the sales-per-size factor, divide the sum of your sales by the sum of the size factor for those three or five years. For example, if your sales to the power-generation industry are $2 million, $2.5 million, and $2.75 million over the past three years and the kilowatt-hours produced over the same period are 1.2 billion kWh, 1.3 billion kWh, and 1.3 billion kWh:

$$\frac{\text{Sales per}}{\text{Size factor}} = \frac{\$7,250,000}{3.8 \text{ bn. kWh}} = \$.0019\text{kWh}$$

Sales-per-Size Factor

Divide your current sales revenue from each customer by the size factor and develop your sales-per-size factor ratio. For example, dividing your current sales revenues by the number of employees at the customer location will yield the sales amount per employee. Enter this figure in column 5.

Industry List

Next, make an industry list. Combine all customers within the same industry and list their industry code or name in column 6. Add their total purchases from you and their size factors. Divide the total purchases by the combined size factor and calculate a sales/size factor typical of that industry and enter this figure in column 7.

In Exhibit 1-1, the sales amount per employee (column 5) represents your current market share and will be an indicator of potential sales to customers with whom you are not currently doing business in that industry (vertical market). As an example, consider that your sales amount per employee ratio for the farm equipment industry is $70. When examining a new potential farm-equipment account with 1,600 employees, you can estimate your sales potential at the new account as $70 x 1,600, or $112,000.

If you're in consumer goods, your sales/size factor may be in dollars per square inch of retail shelf space available or dollars per square foot of wholesale floor space available. Assume that retailers in grocery stores typically consign your product to no more than 1,000 square inches of shelf space, whereas pharmacies may consign no more than 600 square inches. If your sales are $10 per square inch per week, then the grocery would have a potential of $10,000 per week and the pharmacy would have a potential of $6,000 per week.

Develop a list of potential customers in a desired market, by industry, and their size factor. Enter this total size factor in column 8.

Multiply the total-potential-size factor by your sales-per-size-factor ratio for that industry to yield an estimated market potential. Enter this figure in column 9. This is not a forecast, nor a true market potential. It is an estimate only, for use in developing target markets. You still have to get out to the market and interview potential customers in order to verify your estimates.

The Target Market Profile is an extrapolation of your current business into an industry profile that identifies those industries (vertical markets) where you currently have the greatest potential for developing new customers. Eighty percent of all new business comes from current customers or from those industries in which you have a predominant presence—your "core" business. This is only a guideline and does not in any way constitute a forecast. The Target Market Profile merely indicates to you and your distributors those industries and businesses (vertical markets) that contain your most likely sales potential. Once you have completed it, you must travel to the distributors markets to verify that the potential vertical markets actually exist in a particular distributor's market area.

Identifying Target Accounts in Each Market

Once you have determined the vertical markets on which you should concentrate your sales and marketing efforts—those markets with the greatest sales potential—use the sources mentioned on pages 15–18 to identify the potential accounts that fit your Target Market Profile. Also, above and beyond these sources, you may want to talk with business students in local colleges, other businesspeople, and bank officers in a desired market who may be able to offer excellent economic information. The students not only have first-hand market knowledge but may also have access to market research data through their college or university, and they may be willing to work with you on a project basis to earn college credits and/or for a small fee or gratuity.

Contact each of these identified accounts via personal letter advising each of your company, its place in the market, its history, and its strategies for entering the new market. Also, advise these potential customers of your company's stated mission as it will benefit them. In your letter, advise the potential customers as to when and how they will next be contacted by you or an intermediary to discuss a mutually beneficial business relationship.

It is desirable that you travel, if at all possible, to each potential market, as there is really no substitute for the first-hand learning experience you can get by interviewing potential customers and establishing their needs and expectations

Your interviews should be designed to determine how, where, and for what reason the customers buy your type of products, and what market dynamics they anticipate in the near and long-term future. These initial interviews also provide an opportunity to request that these potential customers share their expertise concerning distributors from whom they currently purchase your type of product.

Identify and Analyze Your Competition

From the sources listed on pages 15–18, determine which of your possible competitors currently have market status and how it was earned. See particularly the National Trade Data Bank and the Comparison Shopping Service. Determine also what the market's perception is of your type of products and how they are currently positioned and marketed. "Type of product" implies generic products; for instance, a specialty screwdriver is a hand tool, a custom-designed diamond reamer is a cutting tool, a specially designed and insulated ski jacket is active wear.

In many world markets you will discover that your competition is a functional equivalent rather than a direct competitor. A functional equivalent implies product usage, not a specific product—for instance, mud vs. cement for home construction, abacus vs. calculator or cash register for accounting purposes, courier service vs. state-of-the-art telecommunications for correspondence.

Always remember that all worldwide sales of steel twist drills resulted from the fact that the customer wanted a "hole," not a drill.

Sources of Information Concerning World Markets

Information concerning most world markets is readily available in most major business newspapers and magazines and from a host of private consultants. The business newspapers and magazines are available in most large libraries. A good deal of the information tends to be either of a general "how to do business" nature or pure statistical summaries with no analysis.

The following services supply information concerning distributors and distribution. They are recommended as a starting point for your market research.

U.S. Government Sources

The U.S. Department of Commerce provides extensive information for all types of business. For general information, contact:

> U.S. & Foreign Service
> National Technical Information Service
> 5385 Port Royal Road
> Springfield, VA 22161
> Phone: (703) 487-4650.

Department of Commerce publications are as follows:

1. **National Trade Data Bank (CD-ROM)**
   $360/year
   12 issues/year

   An international trade and economic information catalog of fifteen U.S. agencies, 100,000 documents, import and export statistics broken down by commodity and country, market research reports, over 50,000 trade contacts.

2. **Foreign Trade Report (FT447)**
   Annual.

   Statistical record of exports by type, quantity and dollar value.

3. **Industry Sector Analysis (ISA)**
   $10/report
   Periodic updates

   Reports for one industry in one country giving market size, economic outlook, distribution channels, business customs and practices, competitive situation, trade barriers, business contacts. (Re periodic updates: Unless there has been a large demand, some of these reports could be three years old.)

4. **Market Share Reports**
   $11/country
   Periodic updates

   Basic data on market trends, demands for specific products, U.S. competitiveness versus that of other countries. Also available as Commodity Reports at $10/commodity. Covers 88 countries and more than 400 commodities. (Note: Some of these reports could be three years old.)

5. **Comparison Shopping Service**
   $500/country

   Market research performed by U.S. commercial officers covering marketing factors, names of competitors, comparative pricing, market entry, distribution channels, names of prospective agents, distributors, licensees. (Available for off-the-shelf commercial items only.)

6. **Country Marketing Plan**
   $10/report

   Analysis of marketing conditions in 65 countries and each country's best prospects for U.S. companies.

7. **Foreign Economic Trends (FET)**
   $55 annual subscription or $1/report

   Current business and economic developments and economic trends for 100 countries. Trend reports are prepared annually or semi-annually, depending on the country.

8. **Overseas Business Reports (OBR)**
   Semi-annual

   Projections and outlook for U.S. trade in a specific country. Contain economic and statistical profiles on specific countries and semi-annual reports on the volume and nature of U.S. trade. Available by subscription or individual reports. Price not published.

The U.S. Department of State also provides information for businesspeople. For publications, contact U.S. Government Printing Office, phone (202) 783-3238. The publication *Background Notes*, $14 annual subscription, includes surveys of a country's people, economy, government geography, foreign policy, and trading partners.

The U.S. Agency for International Development's *Congressional Presentations* (telephone (703) 235-1840) lists projects funded overseas by the U.S. government for the coming fiscal year. It also provides information on past funding activities by individual country.

Other U.S. Sources

The following are organizations in the United States that provide information on world markets.

1. Exporter's Encyclopedia
   Dun's Marketing Services
   3 Century Drive
   Parsippany, NJ 07054
   Phone: (800) 526-0651
   $475 including twice per month updates
   Marketing information on 220 world markets.

2. **Statistical Yearbook**
    The United Nations
    Phone: (800) 521-8210
    $85

    Information on imports by country and major exporters thereto.

3. **International Financial Statistics**
    International Monetary Fund
    Publications Unit
    700 19th Street, NW, Washington, D.C. 20431
    Phone (202) 623-7430.
    $148 annual subscription, $15 per individual issue
    12 monthly issues plus yearbook issue and two supplementary reports

    Has information on exchange rates, banking, interest rates, government financing, productivity, and other finance-related topics.

Information From Other Countries

Almost every country maintains a Trade and Development Board in New York City as part of its U.N. mission or in Washington, D.C., as part of its Consular Services. The staffs of these Trade and Development Boards or Missions tend to be extremely helpful. They often have statistical information concerning business in their countries.

For consultations on a foreign country's laws as they affect your business, including employment practices, the environment, copyrights, patents, and banking, the following people have proved to be of invaluable assistance:

Baker & McKenzie,
One Prudential Plaza
130 East Randolph Drive
Chicago, IL 60601
Phone: (312) 861-8000

In England, the Department of Trade and Industry, Victoria Street, Westminster, London SW1.38, is a semi-private branch of the British government that provides a substantial library and reference section for public use. You may also order in-depth specific reports concerning world markets compiled by British government officials and businessmen living and doing business in those markets. Costs are reasonable and the reports are detailed and current.

> The *Economist*
> EIU Research
> 25 St. James Street
> London, SW1A
> United Kingdom
> Phone: (071) 830-7000
> New York City phone: (800) 938-4685

The Economist Intelligence Unit offers many current and concise reports on foreign countries through their weekly magazine, two which are recommended:

1. Investing, Trading & Licensing, $225/report/country, $1,975 for 58 countries
2. Financing Foreign Operations, 225/report/country, $1,595 for 47 countries

Defining Markets by Common Cultures

In past years, many companies have defined world markets by geographic boundaries and appointed managers, agents, and distributors to be responsible for sales within those geographic boundaries. They have signed exclusive agency or distributor agreements determined by, and restricted to, the same geographic boundaries: the so-called territory.

To many companies, these boundaries represented an entire country; a distributor might very well have been an exclusive for France, Germany, or Venezuela. These "country exclusives" were quite popular following the end of World War II, and many are still in existence throughout the world today.

However, in the 1990s very few countries represent a market. Markets are as varied as the cultures within the country. Take Spain, for instance. In consumer goods, the Catalonian market (Barcelona), the Aragon market (Zaragossa), the Castilian market (Madrid), the Andalusian market (Malaga, Cordoba, Seville), the Basque market (San Sebastian, Bilbao), and other provincial markets constitute a region of eight major markets and market cultures. The current European Union, rather than consisting of fifteen countries, constitutes more than forty-five distinct cultural markets for consumer goods and more than twenty-eight distinct markets for industrial goods.

Thus, a consumer market exists where people purchase products, based on the following:

- Shared mores and beliefs
- Historic customs and habits
- Social, gender, and ethnic distinctions
- Economic development and income
- Media and language

An industrial market exists where purchasers have similar requirements for:

- Product quality
- Workmanship
- Service
- Shared technical skills
- Availability of products

It is essential to be aware of cultural differences within any country, and organize your market strategies and distributor networks to best serve these cultural differences. If you were considering a market strategy for sales in Switzerland, how many distributors should you consider? Switzerland is a small country of three distinct languages and cultures: the Germanic culture of Zurich, Basel, and Bern; the French culture of Geneva and Lausanne; and the Italian culture of Locano and Logorano. You would probably need three distributors to service and sell within the three cultures.

The same comparison can be made for many other countries. Motorola had one distributor in Sao Paulo to sell and service its wireless communications products throughout Brazil. But Brazil consists of eighteen cultural markets, thus Motorola wisely changed its marketing strategy from one of exclusive distribution to one of multilevel distribution in order to sell and service to all the key cultural markets of Brazil.

Who is better equipped to assist you in the development and implementation of multilevel strategies than the distributors who have lived, worked, and built their businesses in these specific markets and market cultures?

However, before you can expect to gain this level of distributor cooperation, you need to know who the potential customers are in any market. Beyond knowing who they are, you must have visited with a cross-section of them and determined their product needs, wants, and buying preferences for your type of product(s).

For industrial goods, you must have a profile of the potential clients, recognize their product and service needs, and know whether they prefer to deal directly with you or with a recommended distributor.

In consumer goods, you must know what the buying public looks for in quality, price, and functionality of products similar to yours and where they prefer to buy. Do they look for your type of product in hyper-markets, local town-center retailers, specialty stores, or elsewhere?

Determine what the market seeks in your products. What are the use, modifications, quality standards, labeling, positioning, promotion, guarantees, warranties, and any other market idiosyncrasies required to most effectively sell your products? Your products may have to be tailored to meet these needs, and therein lies one of the most important services a good distributor can offer. The distributor may be able to provide these required tailoring or value-added services more economically than you can and at the same time provide the prestige of local content.

You'll need to market with a sensitivity to the culture. What you say and how you say it when describing your company and its products may be interpreted quite differently in different market cultures. Acronyms, jargon, and idiomatic expressions that are polite in the United States can be misunderstood or thought of as crude or obscene in other cultures. Therefore, it is important not only to know what you want to say but how to say it. This applies to spoken as well as written messages, promotions, and advertising copy.

Astronaut Deke Slayton tells a story of learning Russian

prior to the first space hook-up of the American *Apollo* space-craft and the Russian *Soyuz* spacecraft. "You had to know the nitty-gritty of what the other man was saying. Our superbrains in Washington said we ought to use a computer to translate for us. That was dumb. Computers don't know nuances and idioms. It's like the computer translating from English into Russian an old favorite phrase most of us grew up with. You know, 'The spirit is willing, but the flesh is weak.' Know what you get when it goes through the computer? 'The vodka is strong, but the meat is rotten.' It don't work too good." [1]

In printed or electronic communications, and even in telephone conversations, the physical expression of the message is missing. Intonation, facial expression, and other forms of body language can convey totally different messages from those that are printed or electronically transmitted. Emphasizing Astronaut Slayton's story, there is no substitute for person-to-person business contact.

In person-to-person contacts the spoken language is important. Although the worldwide language of business is primarily English, there is a courtesy in speaking the other person's language. However, if you are not proficient in the other's language, don't embarrass the person and yourself by trying to speak the language.

Many of your prospective distributors will offer translators, but you should hire your own simultaneous translator. Every country has agencies to assist with hiring translators, and it is only proper courtesy that you do so. Also, translation is not a simple matter, and you're best working with translators from the particular countries you are planning to market to. Motorola hired a translator to convey its printed materials into Portuguese for its Brazilian market. The materials came back to Motorola translated into European Portuguese, which has different meanings and connotations from Brazilian Portuguese.

Likewise, hand motions in Japan are considered impolite and even crude. Hands should stay at one's side except for writing and never be placed on the face. The thumbs-up signal is not used in Italy. The sign for OK—placing the thumb and fore-

---

1. From Alan Shepard and Deke Slayton, *Moon Shot* (Atlanta: Turner Publishing, 1994), p. 356.

finger together—is an insult to Brazilians. In language, never use slang expressions or words that could have a double meaning. Most double entendre words or phrases are not translatable.

Sell your company as well as your products. Prestige, history, and company image are very important when entering most world markets. In Asia, your prestige is a matter of face. In Europe, it is a matter of pedigree. In Latin America, it may be machismo. In most world markets, who you are and how you plan to enhance the regional or local economy are more important than what you have to sell.

Know the distribution system preferred in any cultural market. That's what this book is all about. The systems of value-added sales and marketing have been in existence in world markets for much longer than has been the expression "value added." Consumers have often built relationships with specific sales and marketing channels based upon their perceptions of value added—their perceptions, not yours. These perceptions of "value added" are usually based on service, product availability and historic business relationships. Indeed, the distributor channel or distributor-dealer-retailer channel is the value-added channel in most markets.

Summary

Know your vertical markets and the potential customers therein where you are most likely to secure increased business in those markets through the development of your Target Market Profile.

Become familiar with the multitude of informational services available to you for the purpose of identifying potential customers in each vertical market.

Travel to potential markets and develop your market strategies as multilevel plans that complement the culture of the various markets. In today's world markets, your strategies must be market driven and not designed by product orientation, manufacturing, or financial quotas.

Chapter 2
Developing Market Strategies

Once you have identified the markets that hold the greatest
sales potential and have studied the cultures within those markets, you must develop sales and marketing strategies and a
sales plan for entering each market.

Strategies express *what* you plan to do, not *how* you plan to
do it. A strategic sales and marketing plan should include answers to each of the following:

1. What are the historic buying habits of the market? Does
   the market have a history of buying your type of product and, if so, from whom do those buyers prefer to
   purchase?
2. What is product acceptance and use in the market for
   products similar to yours?
3. What advertising and promotion standards are acceptable in the market?
4. What sales channels are available to you?
5. Who are the potential distributors within the market?
6. Is your company organized to support the distributor's
   sales channel?
7. Do you have a profit improvement strategy to present
   to your company's management and your prospective
   distributor?

Each of these seven questions are examined separately, as follows.

Buying Habits of the Market

Why do consumers and industrial companies purchase products similar to yours and for what perceived benefit? The key word here is *benefit*. Neither consumers nor manufacturers will purchase products unless they perceive a substantial benefit from their expenditure of money. Other than basic needs—food, shelter, and clothing—most purchases are made on the basis of perceived benefits.

Businesspeople, worldwide, speak of performing needs analyses of customers and markets when, in fact, they should be talking about "wants" analyses. For example, a consumer in Florida wants a refrigerator to keep her foods fresh; the customer in Siberia wants the refrigerator to keep the food from freezing. The industrial customer in England wants computers capable of being networked in order to enhance productivity and communication; the customer in Togo wants computers merely to simplify accounting procedures. The company in Germany wants machine tools that are numerically controlled, can be centrally automated, and reduce the need for additional workers; the customer in India wants the same machine tool manually operated so it will increase employment and reduce the taxes that the company pays.

You must know how each market perceives the benefits of your products in order to properly promote, position, and sell your product most effectively.

Where does the market prefer to purchase your products? Purchasers of consumer goods may have a preference for the type of store where they expect to find your product available. Is your product best sold through individual retailers who offer a high degree of sales assistance and customer service or do they expect to see your product available through the super-stores and hyper-markets?

Quicksilver, a manufacturer of surf wear and ski wear, surveyed its primary consumers in the 19- to 25-year age group in Spain and France. Quicksilver's original strategy was to concentrate its sales efforts on the larger department stores in these markets. But the survey results implied that Quicksilver concentrate on active wear boutiques rather than the larger stores. The responses that were given by this targeted age group were as follows:

> We want to make our own selections of Quicksilver products. If the products are sold through department stores, where our parents and grandparents shop, they will purchase the clothing as a gift and make the selection based on their tastes in clothing.

The 19- to 25-year-old age group saw Quicksilver products as an expression of its independence and its unique tastes. Quicksilver changed its strategy in Spain and France, and sold only to active wear or sporting wear boutiques, gaining substantial sales volume.

A similar situation presented itself to Polaroid in the United States. In its industrial photography goods, Polaroid desired to initiate a "national accounts" program with some of its larger customers. In a meeting with General Motors, Polaroid proposed equipment-use audits, buy-backs of obsolete equipment, and other incentives to gain the majority share of GM's industrial photography purchases. The Polaroid presentation was positively received until the Director of Contract Administration for General Motors said, "Who are your local distributors? We don't want to carry any inventory." Polaroid was primarily a direct sales organization and did not have sufficient distributors to service GM's ninety-one manufacturing locations. No deal was consummated.

A similar situation arose a number of years ago concerning the Norton Company, a U.S. manufacturer of abrasives. Norton set a strategy to become a direct sales operation and save the discounts and commissions normally paid to distributors and manufacturer's agents. The Detroit automotive market had historically purchased abrasives through local distributors, who would deliver products on a same-day basis, thereby saving the automobile companies inventory costs. But Norton lost market share because the automobile companies were not about to change their purchasing habits.

Product Acceptance

Goods that sell well in one market may not necessarily carry over into another market. A prime example is in the market for high-speed digital telephone switches. In the more developed economies of the West there exists a large market for this equipment. However, following the fall of the Berlín wall, many manufacturers of this equipment were disappointed when Eastern European markets didn't immediately embrace their products.

The reason should have been obvious. There was no communications infrastructure to handle the high-speed switching. The costs of rewiring Eastern Europe was prohibitive, thus a secondary market opened up for wireless communication. Companies that were prepared to offer both wired and wireless communications benefited; those that offered only wired communication lost markets.

Procter & Gamble had to change strategies in Germany and Japan for its disposable diapers. The diapers had to be made biodegradable in order to gain market acceptance, owing to the environmental concerns of potential German and Japanese customers.

You must research each market separately to determine acceptance and use, not of your product but of the product's applications and of the current use of products similar to yours. Then you can develop your sales and marketing strategy based upon acceptance and use in each market.

Advertising and Promotion Standards

If your research on product acceptance and use indicates that a market demand and/or brand recognition must be created, you will need to research what advertising and promotion standards are acceptable in the market and what media are available to you.

Each country has particular laws governing advertising and promotion. In Germany, for example, a company is not allowed to use "comparative" advertising (mine is better than theirs) unless it can show documentation and test results to verify the claim. In Saudi Arabia, women may be shown only in

ads for female products. In some countries you may not advertise a selling price; in others you *must* advertise a selling price.
In many Asian markets you cannot advertise unless your product is available in the market and your ad informs consumers
where they can purchase the product. Therefore, you should
work with an ad agency that knows the laws of the country
whose market you are about to enter and has previous experience and/or presence in that market.

Also, if your product's name is or can be used generically,
you may have difficulty protecting your trademark or copyright. Such names as Hoover, Formica, Xerox, and Kleenex are
considered generic in many countries. For instance, in England,
Ireland and Scotland, and many of the British Commonwealth
countries, no one vacuums a carpet, they "hoover" it. The
Kendall Company thought of using the word *Nappies* for its disposable diapers in those same markets. But diapers are nappies
in this market, and thus the name was not able to be protected.

Media considerations should also be part of your strategy.
What media are most widely used to advertise and promote
your "type" of product—television, radio, newspapers, poster,
handbills, direct mail? For instance, in England television and
newspapers are the most effective methods of reaching many
consumers, whereas in Indonesia the radio is most effective. Industrial products are effectively promoted through direct mail
in much of Europe and South America, however in South
America, direct mail should be sent to potential customers with
a personal cover letter telling the recipient why the mailer has
been sent and what to look for in the package.

Another consideration in your advertising should be the
context level of the market. Simpson International, Inc., an advertising consultant firm, classifies markets by high and low
context. The company defines *high context* as those markets that
respond to nuances and images, nonverbal scenes and events,
music and intonation. In the high-context markets, customers
are expected to respond through their imagination and intelligence to accept your product per se or to learn more about the
product. *Low context* is defined as those markets where consumers want things spelled out—the more detail you can give
them, the more likely they are to respond. Low-context markets
use their intelligence and imagination to dissect and decipher
your ad content before making a buying decision. Simpson In-

ternational claims that Asian and Middle Eastern markets tend to be high context, Northern European and U.S. markets are classified as low context, and Mediterranean and South American markets are in between.

An executive with the advertising agency Young & Rubicam related what happened a number of years ago to illustrate high and low context. Y&R was making a presentation to Daimler-Benz concerning the advertising for Mercedes-Benz automobiles. Describing the prestige factor of the Mercedes in America, he said, light-heartedly, "We buy the star [referring to the Mercedes logo], you throw in the car." His statement was not well received. This was a high-context statement to a group of low-context Mercedes managers.

What is the status of cooperative advertising programs with distributors in the market you are preparing to enter? Most distributors will participate in cooperative advertising programs when the cost of local advertising is shared between the supplier and the distributor. Learn which programs are currently being used by the distributors and the details of the programs' content. Must the distributor attain a minimum level of sales before the co-op program takes effect? Is there a maximum advertising allowance that can be earned by the distributor? Are the distributors given an advertising allowance before advertising, or is the allowance paid only upon proof of advertising? You must answer these questions before devising an advertising strategy.

For all of the above reasons your advertising agency should have a presence, or at least have the experience of working with a corresponding agency in the potential market. The agency should also be equipped to administer cooperative advertising programs on your behalf.

Available Sales Channels

Even though this book is about developing and managing distributor sales channels, you must know which sales channels the market prefers to purchase through and why. Customers will purchase through the sales channel that provides them with their perception of value added. The distributor's sales channel adds value by maintaining an inventory of products for immediate delivery to the customer, thereby reducing the customer's cost of inventory possession. The distributor also offers the customer a variety of products, thus providing a type of one-stop shopping. Further, a good distributor can provide technical service, product modification, assembly, customizing, promotion, and integration of your products with other products in the distributor's inventory.

The customer may, however, prefer to deal directly with you—the manufacturer—for reasons of technical assistance, custom product design, or even prestige. In this case you must be prepared to develop your strategy of sell-through. Sell-through means that you have a physical market presence and it requires that you work jointly with the distributor in market development, product applications development, and consummation of certain sales.

Potential Distributors Within the Distributor Sales Channel

This is probably the most critical part of developing your sales and marketing strategy. The sources mentioned in Chapter 1, particularly the National Trade Data Bank and the Comparison Shopping Service, plus your current distributors and your advertising agency can be helpful in identifying potential distributors. However, there is nothing more effective in identifying good distributors than a survey of potential customers.

The survey of potential customers requires interviewing those potential accounts that you previously identified in your Target Market Profile (see Chapter 1) and that will become the distributor's customers. Your survey should be designed to determine the names of those distributors with whom the market prefers to do business for your type of product.

Your survey should involve a 15 percent cross-section of the potential accounts you have identified. Experience shows that, statistically, the recommendations you receive from these potential customers will vary only minimally beyond what you learn from this cross-section.

Do not—repeat, *do not*—ask the potential customers to rec-

ommend a distributor. You'll probably get the names of their
brothers-in-law or cousins.

Your survey of potential customers can be developed as
follows:

1. Develop a list of qualities that you know a distributor
must possess in order to be successful in selling your prod-
uct(s). For example:

- A high degree of product knowledge
- Technical expertise
- Knowledge of the customer's markets
- Availability of products
- Compatible product mix
- After-sale services
- Frequency of sales calls
- Professional sales people
- Compatible billing practices

2. From this list select no more than six priority items that
you know customers look for. By letter, phone, or preferably in
person, request that the potential customer name distributors
(plural) with whom he or she has worked in the past, or is
working with currently, who meet these needs.

Your interview may be presented something like this:

> "Mr. Monroe, we're interested in obtaining distribution
> for our products in your marketplace and would ap-
> preciate your sharing your knowledge and expertise of
> distributors for this type of product with whom you
> have done business in the past."

Our experience indicates that when you ask people to share
knowledge or expertise, they are complimented and will seldom refuse your interview. From the above list, you may ask,
"Mr. Monroe, of all of the distributors with whom you have
dealt for this type of product, which distributors tend to exhibit
a high level of product knowledge?

3. List the names of the distributors mentioned in the customer's response. Then ask the second question:

"Mr. Monroe, is it important that these distributors display a high degree of technical expertise beyond their product knowledge and understand your use of the product and how it benefits you?"

If the answer is yes, request the names of the distributors who exemplify this high level of technical expertise.

4. Continue this line of questioning for the balance of your questions, each time listing the names of the mentioned distributors who meet or exemplify each of your criteria.

When you have completed your interviews of 15 percent of your potential accounts, you will have a list of those distributors who meet the criteria you believe necessary to successfully sell your product(s). Following your interviews or mail responses, analyze the recommendations of these potential customers. You will find that a small number of distributors have been named repeatedly. These are the distributors with whom the market prefers to do business. You don't have to look elsewhere!

To demonstrate the power of the survey of potential customers, let me give an example. In 1978, W. C. Fath Associates was retained by a major manufacturer of gasoline service station equipment to assist in the identification of service station supply distributors to sell the manufacturer's vapor recovery systems in Southern California, an area stretching from Bakersfield to the Mexican border. State of California business directories listed 256 business classified as service station supply distributors. In our survey of a cross-section of service station owners in the area only eighteen were prominently named by the persons interviewed. Of the eighteen distributors named, the manufacturer signed sales agreements with twelve of them.

When the state legislature mandated that vapor recovery systems must be installed in all service stations before the end of 1980, our client controlled over 70 percent of the market because it had the best distributors. There are more expedient ways to gain distributors, but none are as effective as the survey of potential customers.

Do not advertise for distributors. There are distributors who will respond favorably to your advertisement though they have no intention of ever selling your product. They respond affirmatively only to keep you from entering the market and competing with competitive products that they currently sell.

Organization That Supports the Distributor Sales Channel

This soul-searching matter must be an integral part of devising your sales and marketing strategy. Support of the distributor sales channel requires maximum responsiveness on the part of your distributor support personnel. Is your current company organization equipped to work with and sell through distributors? Your company must embody the following characteristics in order to be successful in managing the distributor sales channel.

Sharing of Information

Are you willing to share company information with distributors concerning marketing strategy, industry strategy, and financial history? The distributors want to know who you are and who they're going to be working with, and with whom they are going to make a substantial investments. Your credibility is important to all of your distributors. Indeed, before presenting products to a distributor, you must present your company.

Are you willing to consider the distributors as an integral part of your total sales and marketing strategy, and more importantly, part of your sales organization? If you consider the distributors merely as customers for your products, then forget about using the distributor sales channel. You won't be successful!

Statement of Policy

As stated above, the distributors want to know who they're working with. What is your distributor policy? We suggest that you prepare a written statement describing your expectations of your distributors and the support they can expect from you. The Statement of Distributor Policy should be concise, not more than two typewritten pages, and suitable for wall display or for engraving onto the inside front and back covers of your product manual. The reason for the statement's visibility should be obvious. The distributor represents many suppliers and products. They don't always remember the policies of each supplier.

The Statement of Distributor Policy should be composed by the sales department, not the company's legal department. The legal department can seldom write anything in two pages. If Legal insists on signing off on your policy statement, that's fine, but you write it.

Joint Market Planning and Survey Input

You should prepare a program of market planning, sales planning, and sales forecasting that will include the cooperative efforts of each distributor.

Joint planning is a personal, one-on-one exercise that involves sharing and developing the information that you and the distributor need to successfully sell your product. Impersonal formats such as business forms and questionnaires, either paper or electronic, should be avoided. After all, the distributor is an integral part of your total sales and marketing effort—a business partner—and you wouldn't send forms and questionnaires to one of your own salespeople.

Joint planning formats should be designed to encourage an interchange of ideas between you and your distributors, and to create a method of evaluating each other's performance toward attainment of agreed-upon sales and operational objectives.

Profit Margin and Discount Justification

Profit Measurement Standards

Setting a strategy of profitability for you and your distributors requires that you implement consistent profit measurement standards, within standard accounting conventions, that are easy to determine, understand, and calculate. (See Exhibit 2-1.)

It is important that you recognize and become familiar with each of the following profit measurements. Remember, the distributor is profit oriented first and product oriented second. Your success in dealing with your distributors depends on your ability to demonstrate your contributions to each of these margins.

When dealing with distributors, consider the five most commonly used profit measurements:

1. *Contribution Margin* (synonyms: Standard Margin, Direct Margin, Operating Margin). The margin obtained by subtracting the distributor's cost of goods sold plus the distributor's variable selling costs from net sales. Variable selling costs are those costs directly related to the sales, promotion, handling, and shipping of the goods sold.

$$\text{Contribution margin} = \text{Net sales} - \text{cost of goods sold} - \text{variable selling costs}$$

2. *Operating Profit* (synonyms: Profit Before Charges, Undepreciated Profit). The margin obtained by subtracting the distributor's fixed costs of doing business (overhead) from the contribution margin. Fixed costs are salaries, benefits, insurance, mortgages, rents, leases, utilities, and other costs that are not proportional to sales but will be allocated to you by the distributor based upon your sales volume with the distributor.

$$\text{Operating profit} = \text{Contribution margin} - \text{fixed costs}$$

3. *Pre-Tax Profit* (synonyms: Net Before Taxes, Net Operating Profit, Net on Sales). The margin obtained by subtracting charges against profits—such as depreciation, loan repayments, current maturing long-term debt—from operating profit.

$$\text{Pre-tax profit} = \text{Operating profit} - \text{depreciation} - \text{current maturing long-term debt} - \text{other charges against profit}$$

Exhibit 2-1. Profit calculations.

Operating Income Data	Currency	%
NET SALES	$110,000	100.00%
Variable costs of sales		
Cost of goods sold	$70,000	
Direct sales expenses	$5,000	
Materials	$500	
Warehousing and handling	$7,500	
Freight in	$1,500	
Delivery	$1,000	
SUBTOTAL	$85,500	77.70%
CONTRIBUTION MARGIN	$24,500	22.30%
(net sales – variable costs)		
Allocated fixed costs		
Salaries	$10,000	
Benefits	$3,000	
Insurance	$1,000	
Prepaid taxes	$1,000	
SUBTOTAL	$15,000	13.60%
OPERATING PROFIT	$9,500	8.60%
(contibution margin – allocated fixed costs)		
Depreciation	$2,000	
Current maturing; LT debt	$1,000	
Other	$1,000	
SUBTOTAL	$4,000	3.60%
PRE-TAX PROFIT	$5,500	5.00%
(operating profit – depreciation – current maturing – other costs)		
MARGIN OF SAFETY		22.45%
RETURN ON INVENTORY INVESTMENT		136.65%

4. *Margin of Safety* (synonyms: Break-Even Margin, Discount Margin, Safety Margin). The margin obtained by dividing the pre-tax profit by the contribution margin. The margin of safety, expressed as a percent, indicates the sales decrease or variable cost increase that could be absorbed without incurring a net loss.

$$\text{Margin of safety} = \frac{\text{Pre-tax profit}}{\text{Contribution margin}}$$

5. *Return-on-inventory-investment*—ROII (synonyms: Return on Sales, Return on Inventory). This ratio is obtained by dividing net sales by the total investment in inventory. The total investment in inventory is the cost of goods sold plus warehousing and handling costs plus freight costs in and out of the distributor's business. It can also be obtained by multiplying the contribution margin by inventory turns.

$$\text{ROI} = \frac{\text{Net sales}}{\text{Total cost of inventory}}$$

$$\text{ROII} = \text{Contribution margin} \times \text{inventory turns}$$

Discount Considerations

Discounts are "earned" by the distributors based on how much they contribute to reducing your variable costs of sales and other out-of-pocket savings in the development of a new market or the servicing of an existing market. You should prepare an audit of your variable costs of sales as though you were selling through a direct sales force.

Then determine what portion of these costs are being defrayed by the distributor. This audit is required to justify your discount structure and may also be used as cost justification to offer different distributors different discounts, based on the out-of-pocket savings to you contributed by the distributors.

Typically, if your pricing allows your distributors a discount of 35 percent, then your variable cost audit should show that the distributor is defraying 35 percent of these costs.

Variable Costs Audit, Annual Costs

Cost of inventory possession	_____ % sales
Inquiry & quotation processing	_____ % sales
Order entry processing	_____ % sales
Invoice processing	_____ % sales
Sales accounting	_____ % sales
Advertising & sales promotion	_____ % sales
Incremental direct sales staff support	_____ % sales
Other variable costs _____	_____ % sales
Total	_____ % sales

The portion of these costs defrayed by the distributor added to the savings to you by not having to place a full-time direct sales person in the distributor's market is your discount justification. Your discount structure must also be sufficient to meet the distributors contribution margin and ROII requirements. If your distributor says to you, "I don't see that the margin on this product is sufficient," is he asking for more discount? No! What the distributor is saying is, "I don't see the product turnover potential to make my contribution margin and ROII based upon the inventory requirements you are requesting." The ratio between contribution margin and ROII and product turnover is:

$$\text{Contribution margin required} \quad = \quad \frac{\text{ROII}}{\text{Est. turns}}$$

If the distributor's contribution margin requirement is 25 percent and the ROII desired is 140 percent, then by transposing the above formula, your inventory plan should be designed to provide annual product turnover of:

$$\frac{1.40}{.25} \quad = \quad 5.6 \text{ turns}$$

What margin of safety do your distributors require? Most distributors will gladly tell you what this margin is; for industrial products it is usual between 15 percent and 20 percent and for consumer goods between 10 percent and 15 percent, how-

ever if they don't know or won't tell you, then ask them for
their planned pre-tax profit.

$$\frac{\text{Pre-tax profit}}{\text{Contribution margin}} = \text{Margin of safety}$$

All of the above profit considerations should be used to develop a profit plan with each distributor to monitor the distributor's inventory control and turnover and measure your direct
contribution to the distributor's profitability.

Chapter 3
Evaluating Channel Profitability

Chapters 1 and 2 discussed market identification and development of market strategies. But, as you know, your strategies must be cost-justified. Entering a new market or developing a new sales channel can be expensive and time-consuming.

These costs must be offset by the sales potential and expected contribution margin available through sales within the new market, or channel, in order to yield the return on investment and minimum profitability dictated by your company's profit plan. Too many sales executives have delivered impressive sales figures and then lost their positions owing to unimpressive profit margins.

Evaluation of channel profitability must take into consideration the following elements of costs:

1. The cost of market entry through the distributor channel
2. The currency and exchange rates needed to ensure profitability
3. The payment criteria needed to ensure a positive cash flow

4. The current costs of inventory possession to support sales in the selected channel
5. The anticipated costs of inventory control and/or inventory consignment to support the distributor sales channel.

You may say, "Profit management is not in my purview. It is the responsibility of our financial people." Don't be naive. Executives are evaluated on profit, not sales!

Cost of Entry

Your budget (see Exhibit 3–1) should consider the following cost factors involved in recruiting, selecting, and hiring a new distributor for any marketplace. Travel to the distributor's market area is essential. In world markets the telephone is not always a good substitute for a personal visit.

Typically, initial costs of entry will be $50,000 to $100,000 and consume six to eight weeks.

Currency Exchange Considerations

Why should currency exchange considerations be integral to evaluating channel profitability? During the 1980s many companies did business in foreign currencies. As protection against currency fluctuations, they devised hedge programs and purchased derivatives of foreign currency futures. (Currency derivatives are basically an investment in futures, wherein one anticipates that the currency exchange rate will either rise or fall against the dollar or other hard currency.)

During the 1990s, many of these companies lost money on their derivative investments and were forced to take charges against earnings and future profits. The damage from derivative trading by major companies currently amounts to billions of dollars.

It is essential that, although you're not expected to be an expert on currency trading, you select a strong international

Exhibit 3-1. Cost of entry worksheet.

MARKET RESEARCH

Fees paid
(market research consultants,
ad agencies, etc.) $_____

Directories & publications $_____

Software
(market research data) $_____

TRAVEL

Market identification
(requiring physical presence
in the market) $_____

Survey of potential accounts
(requiring physical presence
in the market) $_____

Distributor interviews $_____

Distributor selection $_____

DISTRIBUTOR START-UP

Distributor identity program
(mailers, signage, brochures,
catalogs, etc.) $_____

Sales and market planning $_____

Sales & product training $_____

Initial inventory costs $_____

Initial advertising & promotion $_____

OTHER INCREMENTAL COSTS $_____

TOTAL $_____

bank that has a presence in the market you desire to enter or has a history of working with a correspondent bank in that market.

Very few U.S. banks are international in their trading scope and have a presence in world markets. Citicorp, First Chicago, Bank of America, Bank of Boston, Chase Manhattan, and some others qualify as international banks. In England, Barclays Bank and National Westminster are truly international banks with worldwide presence.

You must also decide which currency is going to be used for invoicing your distributors. Most companies deal only in hard currencies such as the U.S. dollar, the British pound, the German deutschemark and the Japanese yen. The currency selected must have a history of stability against other currencies and be readily exchangeable in world markets.

Some companies "bracket" exchange rates. They negotiate a high and low exchange rate, and if the rate broaches these "brackets," current contracts are renegotiated. As an example, the Spanish peseta was recently devalued to meet the exchange rate brackets set by the European Union. Previously the Portuguese escudo, the Italian lire, and the British pound had been similarly devalued. Companies trading within the European Union had to renegotiate contracts and revise their exchange rate brackets.

Many multinational companies also deal in barter. (Bartering is trading in goods in lieu of currency.) General Electric has a group that actively engages in counter trade, or barter, wherein the company receives payment in goods that it then resells to obtain hard currency. For example, GE sells transformers to Ghana and takes payment in cocoa; GE then trades cocoa to Italy in return for leather shoes; the shoes are traded in Sweden for refined tungsten that GE uses to alloy metals for steam and gas turbine blades. Net profit to GE was almost twice what it would have been had they received dollars from Ghana.

Again, you are not expected to be directly involved in these types of transactions, but you should be aware of the effect of exchange rate fluctuations on your company's profitability and be willing to seek professional assistance prior to negotiating any currency agreement with a prospective distributor.

Payment Criteria

All companies want to be paid on time. The cost of outstanding receivables has a negative effect on everyone's cash flow and ultimately on profitability. Your accountants will tell you that receivables past due reduce the value of an invoice by as much as 2 percent per month depending on short-term interest rates.

When dealing with distributors in world markets, payment terms and payment methods must be competitive and advantageous to you and your distributors. Once again, your bank must play an important role is helping you to select a suitable payment method.

Also, you must be aware of the need for proper export/import documentation, which is required to ensure prompt payment from your distributors. A good international bank will know what documentation is required for each country (market) where you are selling through a distributor.

The types of payment plans most commonly used are the open account, time draft, and letter of credit.

Open Account

Definition: An open account is one in which you ship the goods and await payment. All required documentation for import is sent with the sales invoice.

Application: You may choose open account when the distributor is well known to you and has an excellent credit history.

Advantages: Simplicity of documentation and bookkeeping, competitive with the distributor's other suppliers, and low cost.

Disadvantages: You assume all financing and credit risks until payment is received. There is no third party to act in your interest.

Time Draft

Definition: A promissory note drawn on the distributor's bank. You make shipment of the goods and issue the draft and all necessary import documentation through your bank to the distributor's bank. The time draft specifies a time limit, due date for payment, and that documentation is not to be released until the distributor accepts the time draft.

Application: The distributor has a good credit rating and/or history and the extended terms of the time draft are required either to be competitive or to consummate the sale.

Advantages: The draft is evidence of indebtedness and involves an interested third party, the bank. The distributor is responsible for all finance and bank charges.

Disadvantages: You assume all financing and credit risks until the maturity date of the time draft. If the distributor does not pay or is late in paying, the interested third party, the bank, may take collection action on your behalf.

Note: A sight draft is the same as a time draft except that the distributor pays the draft upon receipt of the documentation rather than on a specified date.

Letter of Credit (L/C)

By far the most used form of payment, however there are many different types of letters of credit, all with varying payment and control criteria.

Irrevocable Letter of Credit

Definition: Initiated by the distributor through its bank, payable to you through a bank of your choice. You may request that your bank "confirm" the letter of credit so you can collect directly from your bank rather than from the distributor's bank. The L/C must be specific in terms of the goods to be shipped, parties to the agreement, documents required of each party, payment terms, amount of credit, expiration date of the L/C, means of shipment, and trade terms.

Application: The distributor's credit rating may be excellent, good, poor, or unknown. The L/C is usually issued for first-time sales and, in some countries, L/Cs are a requirement for import sales.

Advantages: You are paid by your bank and your bank handles all documentation. The credit is irrevocable and cannot be altered. Alteration of the credit requires an agreement from both you and your distributor or your failure to comply with the exact terms of the L/C. For instance, a partial shipment of goods—less than the amount specified in the L/C—may void the L/C. The distributor's failure to produce necessary import documentation or to pay shipping costs may also invalidate the L/C. The key to the advisability of using the L/C is that the bank pays no one nor releases any documents until the terms of the L/C are satisfied, to the letter. Insurance rates on the shipment of goods are reduced when an irrevocable L/C is used.

Disadvantages: Documentation must be precise and can be costly for small shipments.

Other Types of Letters of Credit

Revocable: Less costly and more flexible than an irrevocable L/C, but may be modified by

Revolving: your distributor without prior notice to
you. Seldom used in today's markets.

Allows you to withdraw specified
amounts of money at certain specific in-
tervals, such as per month, quarter, etc.
Revolving L/Cs may be either cumula-
tive or noncumulative. Cumu-lative
means that amounts not withdrawn by a
specified time period may be carried forward. Noncumulative means that
amounts withdrawn must be exact and
there is no provision to carry forward
amounts not withdrawn by the date or
time specified.

Standby: As in an irrevocable L/C, it is the issuing
bank's commitment to pay you upon presentation of the specified documents. The
standby letter of credit is an obligation by
the distributor's bank to (1) repay money
borrowed by or advanced to the distributor, (2) to make payment of other
indebtedness incurred by the distributor,
and (3) make payment owing to a default
by the distributor in the performance of an
obligation.

Inventory Control and Consignment Considerations

A major consideration in the evaluation of channel profitability is
the control and cost of inventory. Although your accountants will
list inventory as an asset on the balance sheet, the cost of pos-
sessing inventory is a liability. What is your cost of inventory possession? Exhibit 3–2 is a worksheet you can use to figure this out.

Current Commercial Interest Rate

The current ninety-day commercial interest rate is what the
bank would charge if you were financing your inventory pur-

Exhibit 3-2. Annual cost of inventory possession worksheet.

Current commercial interest rate	11%
Current money market rates available	<u>7%</u>
Lost investment opportunity (11% – 7%)	4%
True cost of money (11% + 4%)	15%
Warehousing and handling costs (percent of sales)	7%
Insurance and taxes on inventory (percent of sales)	4%
Cost of outstanding receivables (percent of sales)	2%

TOTAL ANNUAL COST OF POSSESSION:

15% + 7% + 4% + 2% = 28%

chases via a bank loan. Even though your inventory is financed out of the company treasury, your accountants will use the current interest rate figure to estimate inventory costs.

Current Money Market Rates

If you didn't have your money tied up in inventory, what annual percentage rate could that money earn in the money market?

Lost Investment Opportunity

This is the current commercial interest rate minus the current money market rates.

Warehousing and Handling Costs

This is the cost of giving your inventory shelf space, floor space, and a roof over its head; also, the cost of moving the inventory and handling it for shipment. In the United States today, the average cost of warehousing and handling is 7 percent of sales revenue.

Insurance and Taxes on Inventory

Inventory is considered an asset by your accountants, and assets are taxable and must be insured. As above, in the United States today, this cost amounts to an average of 4 percent of sales revenue.

Cost of Outstanding Receivables

The costs of invoicing and collecting receivables amounts to approximately 2 percent of sales revenue.

As shown in Exhibit 3-2, if your finished goods inventory sat in your warehouse for one year, its value would be decreased by 28 percent. If you are turning inventory (selling it) monthly, your costs of possession would be 28 percent of sales revenue divided by 12, or 2⅓ percent.

When your distributors inventory sufficient quantities of your product to service their markets, your cost of inventory possession is transferred to the distributors. These costs savings to you are part of the cost justification behind the distributor's discount. If your distributor is not stocking, or carrying inventory, but rather working out of your inventory, then the distributor's discount should be lower to cover your cost of inventory possession.

Your inventory planning to support your distributor channel and ensure that sufficient inventory is available to the market must optimize profits both for you, as the supplier, and for the distributor. Optimum inventory for both parties should be calculated as:

$$\text{Optimum inventory} = \frac{(\text{Sales forecast} \times \text{planned contribution margin})}{\text{planned ROII}}$$

For example:

Sales forecast = $100,000
Planned contribution margin = 25 percent
Planned ROII = 140 percent
Optimum Inventory = ($100,000 x .25)/1.40 = $17,857

Inventory planning must be a joint effort between your distributors and your manufacturing and financial management. Inventory management, although complex, may be eased by following a few simple premises:

1. Inventory must be backed up to support the distributors and should consist of only high-turnover products. Low-turnover products should be considered as work in progress and be known to the distributors as having a definitive lead time.

2. Inventory should never be considered an incentive to the distributor to sell more of the product. There are some managers who believe that loading up the distributor with inventory will encourage the distributor's efforts to sell more. That's an out-

Exhibit 3-3. Consignment inventory worksheet.

DISTRIBUTOR DATA:

1. Units of consignment inventory	5,000
2. Value of consignment inventory (distributor's purchase price)	$50,000
3. Average purchase price/unit	$10
4. Distributor's contribution margin/unit	$2

SUPPLIER DATA:

5. Average contribution margin/unit	$3
6. Allocated sales support & advert. expenses	$20,000
7. Annual cost of inventory possession	27%
8. Current commercial interest rate	11%
9. Planned ROII	15%

CONSIGNMENT FINANCING CALCULATION:

10. Supplier's total investment [2 + 6 + (7 x 2*)]	$83,500
11. Supplier's breakeven unit volume (2/5)	$16,700
12. Distributor's required investment (10 x 9)	$12,525
13. Distributor's inventory turns req'd. (11/1)	3.34
14. Amount to be financed [(10 – 12) + (12 x 8)]	$72,353
15. Distributor's monthly payment (14/12 months)	$6,029
16. Distributor's breakeven (units/month) (15/4)	3,015

*Numbers in brackets or parentheses refer to line numbers in the workshop.

moded way of thinking. Seldom does excess inventory encourage the distributor to sell more effectively. Inventory levels should be dictated by market demand and your jointly developed sales forecast.

3. Minimum order quantities are acceptable to most distributors, however they should be reasonable and designed to cover only your variable costs of order processing, not including manufacturing costs. Your variable costs of order processing should be limited to the clerical and/or engineering costs of order entry and to preparing the finished goods for shipment. The minimum order quantity should equal your variable costs divided by your profit plan contribution margin.

For example:

Variable costs of processing one order = $150
Your planned contribution margin = 25 %
Minimum order = $150/.25 = $600

Consignment Inventory

Consignment inventory—allowing distributors to delay payment until they sell the goods—is not recommended, but it may be necessary in certain startup situations where bank financing is unavailable and the costs of initial inventory are beyond the immediate cash means of the distributor. For instance, we worked with a distributor in Poland recently although inventory financing through local banks was nearly impossible. Interest rates were at 41 percent and the banks would not even consider inventory financing without a sustantial commitment of collateral. This was a startup situation in a lucrative market, so the supplier company decided to finance the distributor through consignment inventory.

If consignment is required, use the worksheet shown in Exhibit 3-3 to calculate the true cost of consignment and the distributor's break-even contribution required to yield your desired return on investment.

Summary

The evaluation of channel profitability is too often overlooked by sales managers and other executives when they develop distributor sales channels. Historically, the distributor sales channel has proved to be the most profitable of the many sales channels available, but it can become unprofitable quite rapidly if you don't recognize the factors that create this channel profitability.

Market entry costs can be very high, but they are controllable. Currency and exchange rate considerations, if not understood or handled by a professional, can erode profitability. Implementing the wrong payment strategy can be a negative factor to your company's cash flow and ultimate profit. Poorly devised inventory plans may do more to erode profit, both yours and your distributor's, than any other marketing factor, with the exception of competitive under pricing or failure to gain market share.

Many sales managers have said to us, "This profit stuff is up to our finance people. I'm paid to sell!" That may be so, but the managers who make it up the corporate ladder are those who understand and control profit.

Chapter 4
Legal Considerations in Distributor Relations

This section explores your legal exposure in dealing with distributors and attempts to make you aware of when you should seek legal assistance. It is not our intention to provide counsel or to make you a legal expert, but merely to raise your awareness of the law as it affects your day-to-day management of the distributor sales network.

It is highly recommended that you have written sales agreements with each of your distributors and that they be modified to meet the laws of the distributors' market areas. Many companies state that their agreements will be adjudicated by the laws of the company's country or state. In many markets, this is not always wise and/or acceptable. For instance, U.S. law is much more restrictive than the laws of many other countries where you will have a distributor. Conversely, laws dealing with distributor relations in most Arab nations and in India are often more restrictive than U.S. laws.

When negotiating your sales agreement with a distributor, make certain that you know the parties to the agreement. In many countries, distributors may be part of a holding company or another financial consortium that acts as a silent partner, or they may be a subsidiary of an unnamed nonfinancial partner.

Recently, we held negotiations with an Eastern European distributor who was partially owned by the government, a fact not made public. We learned of this government ownership through an interview with a local banker while negotiating letters of credit. In this instance, we wanted to avoid the possibility of interference in our distributor relations by some government bureaucrat or agency. No contract was negotiated with the distributor.

Sales Agreement Checklist

Following is a checklist of items to be included in your sales agreement.

☐ Define all parties to the agreement.
☐ Define the term or duration of the agreement. (Current thinking among most attorneys is that the term of the agreement be three to five years, and should be renegotiated annually. The annual renegotiation will include a forecast, market plan, inventory plan, and tactical sales plan to be made part of and included in the sales agreement.)
☐ Negotiate and describe the distributor's principal sales area— that market area where you will measure, evaluate, and support the distributor's sales effort. The principal sales area does not have to be geographic! It can be described as a market segment, an industry, a class of trade, or even a specific list of customers.
☐ Identify the duties of the distributor.
☐ Identify the duties of your company in supporting the distributor.
☐ Identify the products to be sold. The product mix may be selective and different for different distributor markets.
☐ List the prices at which the distributor may purchase products.
☐ Define your delivery and shipping terms.
☐ State your returned goods and/or obsolescence policy.
☐ State your payment and credit terms.

- ☐ Negotiate and define the distributor's inventory requirements.
- ☐ State your sales promotion and advertising policy with particular reference to your co-op advertising program requirements.
- ☐ Define your product guarantees, warranties, copyright, and patent infringement policy.
- ☐ State the terms and conditions for terminating the agreement; that is:

  — Failure to perform to agreed-upon sales and marketing plans and goals
  — Misrepresentation or misapplication of your products
  — Misuse or misapplication of your trademarks or logos
  — Failure to maintain credit-worthiness
  — Insolvency
  — Conviction for violating the country's laws
  — Change of ownership of the distributor

"Evergreen" agreements—those without a termination date or "without cause" termination terms—are not acceptable in many countries. Many legal counselors also advise against these open-ended, no duration agreements. In the European Union, for instance, an agreement that is open-ended and not renegotiated within a five-year period becomes an exclusive agreement and qualifies the distributor to seek severance payments upon termination of the agreement.

Exclusive vs. Nonexclusive Agreements

In the United States, an "exclusive" agreement is interpreted as a condition that you place upon yourself not to appoint another distributor in your current distributor's market area.

In the European Union, however, an exclusive agreement means that the distributor has an exclusive right to sell in the defined principal sales area and may not solicit business outside of the principal sales area. Notice the word *solicit*. The law does not prevent the distributor from *selling* outside the principal sales area. Exclusive agreements carry with them the distributor's right to seek severance upon termination.

Most counsel suggest nonexclusive agreements, however

the culture of most distributors desires some form of exclusivity. Therefore, the U.S. interpretation of exclusivity by the supplier may be written into your nonexclusive agreements. This usually satisfies the distributor culture in many countries. For example:

> The company agrees not to appoint another distributor in the defined principal sales area provided that the distributor performs to the sales and marketing plans as set forth herein.

Registration and Licensing

In most Arab nations and some South Asian and East Asian countries, a distributor must be registered and licensed to sell specific products. In most Arab countries this registration also carries the requirement that the distributor be a "national," or a bona fide citizen of the country; further, the laws stipulate that the distributor's business be 51 percent owned by other "nationals."

It is the responsibility of you, the supplier, to ensure that your distributor is properly licensed.

European Union Laws Governing Distributor Relations

The basis of the law governing businesses and distributor relations in the European Union is the 1957 Treaty of Rome. The following are some pertinent articles of that law and how they affect the supplier-distributor arrangement.

Article 85(1)

This section prohibits any agreements or practices between two or more enterprises that restrict competition within the European Union (EU) and affect trade between the member states of the EU.

Provisions in distributor agreements deemed restrictive are

exclusivity grants, noncompetition clauses, territory restrictions, and reciprocal agreements between competing manufacturers to act as distributors for each other. This restriction has been expanded to include a manufacturer's affiliates or subsidiaries that manufacture competing goods.

Article 85(3)

This permits the promulgation of exemptions to Article 85(1) for agreements that are deemed to be pro-competitive and contribute to, and enhance, the production or distribution of goods and/or promotes technical or economic progress.

This means that companies and/or their distributors may petition the court to form joint ventures and alliances that, although they may violate Article 85(1), would be in the best pro-competitive interest of the EU.

Regulation 67/67 (1967)

This was the original European Commission exemption to Article 85(1), made available to companies in their distributor agreements. It granted exclusive distributor agreements to parties that met de minimus guidelines. The de minimus guidelines were stated as follows: "applies to agreements where the combined annual sales of the parties to the agreement, including all of their subsidiaries and affiliates, were less than 50 million ECUs and where the market share of the combined parties to the agreement was less than 5 percent within the EU."

Regulation 1983/83 (1983)

This replaced Regulation 67/67 regarding exclusive distributor agreements and allowed the following permissible restrictions:

• *Noncompetition clauses.* The distributor may be restricted from manufacturing or distributing products competitive to yours only for the term of the sales agreement and without extension beyond termination of the agreement.

• *Export sales.* The distributor may be restricted from soliciting products outside of his principal sales area and/or maintaining a branch or warehouse outside of the principal sales area. It is not permissible to restrict the distributor from selling unsolicited products outside of the principal sales area within the European Union.

• *Minimum purchases.* The distributor may be required to purchase your full line of products and may be required to adhere to minimum purchase quantities.

• *Trademarks and logos.* The distributor may be required to sell your products under your trademarks and logos or packed and presented to your specifications.

• *Advertising and promotion.* The distributor may be required to advertise and promote your products to your specifications and within your guidelines, maintain a trained sales force or sales network for your products, keep an inventory of your products, employ a staff having specialized or technical training for your products, and promote your products in a manner consistent with the image you desire to put forth to the market.

• *After-sale service.* The distributor may be required to offer after-sale service and warranty and/or guaranty service.

• *Direct sales.* In return for a noncompetition clause or an exclusive purchase agreement, the distributor may request, and obtain by law, a "no direct sales" clause from you, the supplier.

• *Territory.* Under this regulation, you may now grant a distributor exclusivity for the entire European Union.

• *Intra-brand competition.* Regulation 1983/83 prohibits restraints on the resale of your products, which adversely affects the availability of your products to other purchasers (distributors, dealers, retailers, consumers, etc.). For example, suppose you restrict the distributor's resale of automotive oil filters only to be sold to full-service garages, thereby making your oil filters unavailable through other market channels.

• *De minimis guidelines.* Regulation 1983/83 raised the monetary value of the guidelines from 50 million ECUs to 200 million ECUs. Therefore, to be included in the block exemption from Article 85 (1) of the Treaty of Rome, your company plus all of its subsidiaries and affiliates and the distributor and any of its subsidiaries and affiliates must not have combined annual sales revenues, worldwide, of more than 200 million ECUs. (Currently an ECU is about $1.04.)[1]

Regulation 1984/83 (1983)

This regulation deals with exclusive purchase agreements for nonexclusive distributors. If you extract a noncompetition agreement from a nonexclusive distributor and designate a principal sales area, the distributor has the right to demand and obtain a "no direct sales" clause. Further, the nonexclusive distributor, under an exclusive purchase agreement, may *not* be restricted from solicitation outside of his principal sales area. This differs from an exclusive distributor agreement, wherein the distributor *may* be restricted from solicitation of sales outside of its primary sales area.

Exclusive purchase agreements may *not* exceed a duration of five years. European Union law is, for the most part, written by the European Commission and adjudicated by the European Court of Justice, which sits in Brussels. As with U.S. antitrust law, there are no precedents in EU Law. The ECJ decides cases based upon competitive impact at the time of a violation of current law. European Union law regarding competition policy applies not only to the fifteen member states of the union but also to those member states of the European Free Trade Area. This merger of law has created the European Economic Area (EEA).

U.S. Law Governing Distributor Relations

The Sherman Antitrust Act (1890)

The basis of the laws governing businesses and distributor relations in the United States is the Sherman Antitrust Act, Section I. The Sherman Act is the "grandfather" of all business law in the United States, and has been stated by the Supreme Court to be second in importance only to the Constitution. It has been copied by major industrial nations around the world. The

---

1. As of this writing, the European Court of Justice is considering a petition, from the Council of Ministers, to raise the 200 million ECU guideline to 300 million ECUs.

Treaty of Rome and the Australians, Japanese, and the Filipinos
have all used "Sherman" as a basis for their antitrust laws. The
Sherman legislation was enacted in 1890 to make illegal the car-
tel actions of American oil, steel, lumber, railroad, and banking
industries. The Sherman Act states:

> Every contract, combination in the form of trust or oth-
> erwise, or conspiracy, in the restraint of trade or com-
> merce among the several States, or with foreign
> nations, is declared to be illegal. Every person who
> shall make any contract or engage in any combination
> or conspiracy declared by this title to be illegal shall be
> deemed guilty of a felony, and, on conviction thereof,
> shall be punished by fine not exceeding one million
> dollars if a corporation or, if any other person, one
> hundred thousand dollars or by imprisonment not ex-
> ceeding three years, or both said punishments, in the
> discretion of the court.

The provision of the law was that it be enforced by the Executive Branch of the U.S. government and adjudicated by the
U.S. Department of Justice. Current recommendations to the
Department of Justice (1994) by Congress is that the maximum
fine for a corporation be raised to include "total pecuniary damages" resulting from a violation of the law and that the three-
year felony conviction carry with it a mandatory period of
confinement. This is a strong recommendation and not to be
taken lightly. In 1993, 161 company executives were convicted
under Sherman I; more than half of those executives served jail
terms.

As companies and businesspeople, we all participate in
contracts and combinations with customers, distributors, and
vendors, with the intent to limit competition. Are we then in violation of the law? No, because since the law's inception the
Supreme Court has interpreted it to mean, "Every unreasonable
contract, combination . . . in restraint of trade."

What is an unreasonable restraint? The first and foremost
unreasonable restraint is price fixing. That's when you and your
competitors decide to do something in collusion to effect resale
prices.

Price fixing is seldom blatant. A statement at a trade association meeting that profits are eroding and prices must be increased can be considered price fixing if the industry adheres to this "invitation to take collective action." An agreement not to deal with customers who are more than sixty days past due in their remittances has been considered, by the courts, as a collusive act that violates the law. A joint refusal to bid, taking turns on bids, and comparing bids are all cases of price fixing.

Likewise, the allocation of customers is illegal. If you say, "I'll stay away from your Motorola business if you stay away from my Intel business," that violates the law. So is the allocation of territories. To say, "I'll stay out of Michigan if you stay out of Ohio" violates the law. The same is true of the allocation of products. "Let's all agree to use only 25 percent Durham wheat in our semolina" violates the law.

The cardinal rule for "Sherman" is, Don't talk to your competitors. You can't violate the act unilaterally.

A violation of the law between companies at the same functional level—that is, manufacturer-manufacturer, distributor-distributor, retailer-retailer—is called a horizontal violation and deemed to be illegal per se, meaning "on its face." There is no defense for a per se violation of the law. Once the Department of Justice impanels a grand jury and issues its subpoenas, there is no defense and the courts will not allow a nolo contendre plea. (Nolo contendre has been used in the past to say, "I will not contest the court, but I also will not plead guilty.") A nolo contendre plea may carry with it a conviction, but because there is no plea of guilty, there is no permanent record of your conviction. Forget it! If the grand jury determines that you have violated Sherman I, you're guilty.

A vertical violation of the law occurs when there is collusion in a vertical channel—that is, manufacturer-distributor-dealer. An agreement to set resale prices or to do anything that adversely affects resale price, in collusion, is per se illegal. Agreements to allocate sales territories, products, and customers also violates the law, however the Supreme Court has said that you may have a pro-competitive reason for these collusive acts and the Court will hear your defense under the doctrine of the Rule of Reason.

The Rule of Reason was written by Justice Byron White in a 1977 case involving Continental TV, a San Francisco retailer, and GTE-Sylvania. Continental was restrained by GTE-

Sylvania from opening a sales branch in Sacramento. The Supreme Court ruled in favor of GTE-Sylvania, and Justice White wrote that the law was intended to encourage inter-brand competition, not intra-brand competition, and that there may be a pro-competitive reason for discouraging intra-brand competition among the resellers of a company's products.

In the United States, once you have sold your goods to a distributor, they are no longer yours and you have no control, through agreement, over the price of the goods, where they are sold, or to whom they are sold. You may have some control over where and to whom your products are sold if you can show that the sale of your products to a particular class of trade or to a particular customer could be detrimental to "public health and safety." This is referred to as the "Wella" exclusion to the law.[2] For instance, if you are the manufacturer of control valves, you may be able to show that indirect sales to the nuclear power industry may be detrimental if the sale is made without specific technical knowledge.

There is one other, seldom used, exception to a vertical price-fixing violation, referred to as the Colgate doctrine, named for the company now known as Colgate, Palmolive-Peet. The Court was asked to review Colgate's policy of publishing and pre-ticketing resale prices. The Court decided that "You could state your policy (re published resale prices) and no more." "No more" means that you cannot encourage, entice, conspire, or counsel with your customers to maintain your price policy.

A case in point concerning the Colgate doctrine involves Cuisinart and Russell Stover Candies. Russell Stover had a policy of pre-ticketing resale prices. The company would send its salespeople around to retailers and determine which retailers

2. The Wella exclusion is so named because of a case involving Wella hair products. Wella had two channels of distribution. One channel consisted of distributors who were authorized to sell Wella concentrates to licensed beauticians. The other channel consisted of distributors who sold Wella products to retailers.

Some of the distributors who sold only the Wella concentrates decided to reblend and private label the Wella concentrates and sell them in competition to Wella's products. Wella sought a court injunction to prevent the distributors from private labeling. The distributors cried, Restraint of trade! The court ruled for Wella in the interest of public health and safety, stating that The distributors were not qualified to blend the concentrates and by so doing could cause damage to the hair or skin of the consumer.

were discounting pre-ticketed prices. Those retailers who were discounting would be refused orders for Russell Stover products. Cuisinart had the same policy, however there was evidence that Cuisinart had counseled its retailers to bring prices up to the pre-ticketed retail levels. Both cases were heard in U.S. District Court, in Hartford, Connecticut, by the same judge. Russell Stover was exonerated because it did "no more." Cuisinart was found guilty of violating the law because it "counseled with [its] customers."

Another case involved Dart Drug stores in Virginia and Maryland. Parke-Davis Pharmaceuticals stood by the Colgate doctrine and stated that it would not deal with discounters of its posted resale prices. Dart Drugs received a shipment of Parke-Davis products and discounted them, despite the company's policy. In response, Parke-Davis refused to supply its products to Dart Drugs, which was totally within its right under the Colgate doctrine. However, Parke-Davis made a mistake. Dart petitioned Parke-Davis to resupply their stores with products, promising not to discount. Parke-Davis honored Dart's request and after receiving the products Dart immediately discounted. Parke-Davis refused products to Dart the second time. Dart sued Parke-Davis, through the Department of Justice, claiming that Parke's actions were based upon Dart's promise to "fix" resale prices. Dart won a substantial settlement.

The lesson to be learned from *Dart* v. *Parke-Davis* by all who sell through distributors is that once you have terminated a distributor, never rehabilitate that distributor.

The Clayton Act (1914)

Whereas the Sherman Act addresses collusive acts and practices, the Clayton Act deals with discriminatory practices and artificial barriers to trade. The Clayton Act established the Federal Trade Commission (FTC), which adjudicates the law. The two sections of the act that concern relations with distributors are Sections 2 and 3.

The penalty for a violation of the Clayton Act is a misdemeanor; however, the law allows the plaintiff to seek treble damages (three times proven financial injury), court costs, and reasonable attorney's fees (which never are).

Section 2

Section 2 of the Clayton Act deals with discriminatory business practices in dealings with distributors. It prohibits discrimination in prices of goods supplied to competing distributors, wherein the result of such discrimination causes injury to competition. For example, if you sell to distributor A at $1.00 and to distributor B at $1.20, and distributor B can show that your discriminatory prices have injured his business, you have violated the law.

Section 2 also deals in services offered to competing distributors, wherein offering disproportionate services to one distributor and not to the competing distributor may be ruled as unlawful if the unfavored distributor can show injury to his business.

As originally written, the act stated that there would be no discrimination in prices charged to competing customers in the sale of goods of "like grade and quantity." The word *quantity* provided a large loophole for suppliers of chain stores, which was coming into being during the 1920s. Therefore, Section 2 of the act was amended in 1936, and *quantity* was changed to quality. This amendment is known as the Robinson-Patman Act.

The Robinson-Patman Act

The Robinson-Patman Act consists of six sections, 1a through 1f. However, because this law is an amendment to the Clayton Act, Section 2, these sections are usually referred to as 2a through 2f .

Section 2a

Section 2a declares price discrimination to be unlawful, but states that seven factors must exist before a violation of the law can occur: There must be price discrimination in sales to: (1) two or more purchasers of (2) commodities (tangible goods) of (3) like grade and quality, (4) in commerce (physically across State lines), (5) sold for use, consumption or resale, (6) where the effect of such discrimination may (7) substantially lessen competition, create a monopoly, or cause injury to, destroy, or prevent competition.

Section 2a further states:

> That nothing herein contained shall prevent differentials which make only due allowance for differences in the cost of manufacture, sale, or delivery resulting from differing methods or quantities in which such commodities are to such purchasers sold or delivered.

This is known as the cost-justification defense to a price discrimination violation of the law. It states that you may offer a discriminatory lower price to a distributor if you can "cost-justify" the lower price through showing that the distributor has provided quantifiable cost savings to you in the sale or delivery of your products. If one of your distributors is taking deliveries in larger, less freight-expensive quantities and is actively selling, promoting, and advertising your products; holding sufficient inventory to meet market needs; and maintaining an active, well-trained sales force whereas another competing distributor is providing less of these services, you may have a cost justification to offer each distributor different prices.

Although the law specifically cites manufacturing cost saving as a justification, the courts have, since the inception of the law, disallowed the manufacturing cost justification. Their reasoning has been that the lower price offered for large quantities or a longer production run were made possible by the higher prices being charged to the smaller buyer.

Does the above mean that you cannot offer a quantity discount? The courts have realized the need for incentive discounts to encourage distributors to purchase in larger quantities; however, the courts have also ruled that whatever incentive discount you offer must be reasonably available to all of your distributors.

For example, suppose you offer an incentive discount schedule as shown:

100 units	1 percent discount
200 units	2 percent discount
300 units	3 percent discount
500 units	5 percent discount

All of your distributors must be reasonably able to purchase 500 units. If only one or two of your larger distributors can reasonably purchase 500 units, the difference between the unit volume that can be reasonably purchased by all distributors and your 500 unit discount must be cost justified.

In the following paragraph of this section, the FTC is given investigatory power to ensure that quantity discounts are fair and reasonably available to all purchasers:

> [W]here it [FTC] finds that available purchasers of greater quantities are so few as to render differentials of account thereof unjustly discriminatory or promotive of monopoly in any line of commerce [the FTC may impose quantity discount limits].

The law does not apply to discriminatory prices charged where there is an imminent deterioration of goods, obsolescence of seasonal goods, distress sales under court process, or sales made in the good-faith discontinuance of business.

Section 2b

This section is called the "good faith meeting of competition" defense. The law states:

> that nothing herein contained shall prevent a seller . . . showing that his lower price or offering of services or facilities to any purchaser or purchasers was made in good faith to meet an equally low price of a competitor. . . .

Section 2c

This section makes it unlawful for any agent or broker to offer or pass through to the purchaser, or for the purchaser to receive, any portion of the agent's or broker's duly earned commission or fee in order to obtain a favorable or discriminatory price for the purchaser. This law was written to stop the practice by A&P Foods and others of demanding that their suppliers lower the prices charged by giving A&P the amount of money that would normally be paid to a broker or agent as a sales commission.

Section 2d

This section states that any promotional allowance paid to a purchaser, or anything of value given to the purchaser, in connection with the processing, handling, sales, or offering for sale the products of the seller must be offered to all purchasers competing in the distribution and sales of the products on proportionately equal terms.

Section 2e

Essentially the same as Section 2d, Section 2e deals with services and facilities offered to competing purchasers who buy for resale. Sections 2d and 2e can be easily adhered to by setting, as a matter of policy, the proportionality of all promotional allowances and services available to all of your distributors. For instance, the agreement could state, "The distributor may earn an allowance of $1.00/unit sold over and above the first 500 units sold in any calendar year."

Section 2f

This section states:

It shall be unlawful for any person engaged in commerce, in the course of such commerce, knowingly to induce or receive a discrimination in price which is prohibited by this section.

These six sections of Robinson-Patman were written to protect the small retailer and distributor. The Federal government through the FTC and the Department of Justice has not actively enforced these laws since 1974. However, states attorneys general and civil litigants have crowded the courts with Robinson-Patman lawsuits. As of this writing, there are over 1,300 Robinson-Patman suits pending.

Basic Law Clayton Act, Section 3

This portion of the act prohibits "exclusive dealing," wherein the condition of sale is that:

> [T]he purchaser thereof shall not deal in the goods, etc. of a competitor or competitors of the seller and where the effect of such an agreement may substantially lessen competition or create a monopoly.

The FTC and the courts have read into this law other practices beyond exclusive dealing that are considered artificial barriers to trade and commerce. To wit:

• Tying arrangements, making the condition of sale that the purchaser buy one product or service as a condition for buying another product or service. For instance, "If you want to sell my copier, you must buy my toner." Forget it!

• Reciprocity, making the condition of a sale or purchase contingent on an exchange of products and/or services between the buyer and seller. For example, "You purchase my tires, I'll ship goods only in your trucks." Forget it!

• Total requirements contract, making it a condition of sale that the purchaser buy all of its requirements for your products solely from you. When dealing with distributors, total requirements contracts are sometimes referred to as "full line forcing."

• Predatory pricing, described as pricing at or below cost with the intent to injure competition. If the FTC or Department of Justice believes that your pricing policy in one market or to one class of trade is below what you are pricing in other markets, and your intent is to gain market share by driving out competition, you may be guilty of predatory pricing.

What is "at or below cost"? If your actual cost is $1.00 and you sell at $1.10, you may be at or below cost. The courts will look at your industry and decide what level of contribution margin is required to cover your fixed expenses. If, for instance, the industry average contribution margin is 25 percent, then the formula used to calculate cost is as follows:

$$\frac{\text{Actual costs}}{1 - \text{industry average contribution margin}} = \text{minimum selling price}$$

In the above example:

$$\frac{\$1.00}{1 - .25} = \$1.33$$

This is the minimum selling price required to break even. Selling at or below $1.33 could, therefore, be deemed as "at or below cost."

In all of the above cases there must be a substantial impact on the lessening of competition or tending to create a monopoly. However, there is one more act than can be invoked if the FTC thinks that there is a possibility of lessening competition, Section 5 of the Federal Trade Commission Act.

Basic Law. Section 5, Federal Trade Commission Act

This part of the law reads as follows: "Unfair methods of competition in or affecting commerce, and unfair or deceptive acts or practices in or affecting commerce, are declared unlawful."

That's it. The entire law. Thus the FTC can take what it refers to as prophylactic action to prevent a violation of the law.

Section 4 of the Clayton Act and Section 15 of the Sherman Act as amended in 1975, the Antitrust Improvements and Penalties Act, allow for private suits. Plus, all the U.S. states have antitrust laws administered by their attorney generals. In the recent past, the Department of Justice and the FTC have not aggressively pursued antitrust violations, however the courts are full of state and private actions.

For these reasons and reasons of ethical conduct, it is recommended that you implement an affirmative antitrust program in your company to teach all executives who have the opportunity to deal with customers, distributors, and competitors, so they know the elements of antitrust laws.

Laws of Other Countries Governing Distributor Relations

Each country has some form of law or regulation intended to protect distributors. These laws and regulations concern termination, agency, repatriation of funds, advertising, copyrights, warranties, liability, and import documentation.

Suffice it to say, there isn't the space here to discuss each country's legislation regarding distributors; however, you should make an effort to learn the laws of each country as they affect distributor relations. The best source of information is the consulate of the country or, as stated previously, an international law firm such as Baker & McKenzie.

See Appendix A for information about current laws in various countries.

Chapter 5
Ten Steps for Selecting the Right Distributor

The previous chapters have dealt with the knowledge required to effectively begin your distributor selection process. What follows is a step-by-step process for distributor selection.

For over twenty years we have been helping companies select their distributors, and we know of no better method than the one described here. The ten-step process outlined below requires approximately six to eight weeks per distributor to be selected.

Surely there are more expedient methods, however expediency can be costly and time-consuming. If you have selected the wrong distributor, there is no end to the damage that can be done to your image and reputation in the market. And attempting to terminate a distributor because you have made the wrong choice can result in demands for severance and other forms of payment, and possibly end in a lawsuit, neither of which is desirable.

The ten steps are these and each step will be developed in detail.

1. Identify the market and the potential customers therein.

2. Perform a survey of the potential customers to determine from which distributors they purchase your type of products.
3. Develop your distributor selection criteria and hold screening interviews with prospective distributors.
4. Personally interview all interested distributors and begin your distributor selection process.
5. With the selected distributor, develop your distributor's sales forecast.
6. Negotiate the distributor inventory plan.
7. Negotiate your distributor sales agreement.
8. Implement your distributor identity program.
9. Initiate sales and product training for the distributor's sales force.
10. Develop your tactical sales plan with the distributor's sales management.

Step 1. Identify the Distributor's Market Area

As discussed in Chapter 1, market area identification is incumbent upon you, the supplier. All major accounts in the distributor's market area should be identified by you. Of course, there will be many smaller accounts that will not be known to you, but you must know which major accounts represent your market potential.

The Target Market Profile (Exhibit 1-1) should be your guide to market analysis when using the sources of information described in Chapter 1. The Target Market Profile is intended to provide information on your key vertical markets. Once you have defined these vertical markets, the potential accounts can be easily identified, using the sources mentioned in Chapter 1.

Step 2. Perform a Survey of Potential Accounts

This procedure was discussed in Chapter 2.

Step 3. Develop Distributor Selection Criteria and Hold Screening Interviews With Prospective Distributors

Your selection criteria should be designed to answer the following questions.

1. What market does the distributor serve and what does it consider to be its market niche? Most distributors will openly discuss their market niche—that part of the market where they have had the greatest success and are most comfortable. Discussions with distributors should evaluate how the company defines its market in terms of vertical markets, key customers, and geography.

Also, how does the distributor position his business to the market in terms of products and services offered? For instance, does the distributor say, "We're a pump distributor," or "We're a fluid handling distributor"? Which sounds more professional to you?

2. What is the size of the sales force? How large is the distributor's total sales force, including inside and outside personnel? Better distributors, worldwide, believe that they need at least one inside salesperson for each four outside persons.

Are the outside sales people employees or commissioned agents? You may find that commissioned agents are more difficult to work with than distributor sales personnel.

How are the salespeople assigned responsibilities and apportioned in the marketplace? What does the distributor believe to be his share of market against local competition?

What type of compensation plan does the distributor use for sales personnel? We have found that better distributors tend to move away from straight sales commissions and into more professional forms of profit compensation in order to encourage account development and not just take orders. Also, profit compensation encourages the sales of those products that are most profitable to the distributor, not the easiest to sell.

3. How does the distributor finance inventory? Does the distributor have a commercial credit line available or does he finance from his own treasury? What does the distributor believe

to be an acceptable level of inventory turnover, inventory to sales ratio, and return on inventory investment?

Does the distributor have the necessary physical facilities to handle, store, ship, and support your product line or will additional capital investment be required to properly support your product line? What does the distributor believe should be the minimum level of inventory for your products to support the market?

4. What is the distributor's product line depth and breadth? How many product lines does the distributor inventory and sell (breadth)? How does the distributor control the number of products in a product line (depth)?

Is the distributor's current product mix complementary, supplementary, or competitive with yours? Complementary means that your products could be sold with the complementary product. Supplementary means the supplemental product may be sold with yours. Competitive means that the distributor can offer the customers a wider range of choices.

Some companies have a policy of not dealing with distributors that carry competing product lines. This may be an ill-advised strategy. If the market prefers to purchase your type of product from a specific distributor, you may be losing sales by not dealing with the distributor who carries a competitive line. When a dominant distributor can offer competitive products, the market grows as the distributor can offer more choices and products to his customers. Instead of having your slice of the pie become smaller, in a competitive situation the pie itself gets bigger.

5. What are the distributor's credit reporting procedures? What credit reporting is required by the distributor's other suppliers and the distributor's bankers? Does the distributor file annual, semiannual, or quarterly financial reports to them?

What are your credit reporting requirements and are they compatible with the distributor's current practices? Are you prepared to show how your credit reporting requirements will benefit your ability to support the distributor?

Remember, in many world markets credit reports are either unavailable or considered confidential information. You may have to substitute business and bank references for credit reports. Also, in Brazil and other South American countries, a credit request may be considered an insult to the distributor's integrity.

6. What are the distributor's sales strategies? What are the distributor's views on joint sales and market planning and forecasting?

How many months or years in the future does the distributor believe forecasting is necessary, and how often does the distributor forecast and for what purposes? What market indicators does the distributor use in forecasting and planning? Whatever the distributor considers an important indicator, it must become important to you also.

Consider the following example. A number of years ago, we worked with a distributor of metallurgical graphites who sold primarily to the steel industry in southeastern Michigan. On Mondays, the owner would drive through the areas around the mills and notice how many people were sweeping their front porches or stoops. That meant that the mills had worked over the weekend and their graphite supplies would be low.

In another instance, a distributor of agricultural chemicals in southeastern Indiana had his warehouse in his barn and inside he had a porta-cabin for an office. In the office were him and his secretary and three unoccupied desks. On the wall were three hand-drawn thermometers containing different levels of red color. One would assume three desks, three thermometers, three salesmen and the thermometers were a sales record. Wrong!

When we first met the distributor, he stated that he was expecting an important phone call and would have to interrupt our interview when the call came through. About ten minutes into the interview the phone rang and the distributor asked to be excused. As courtesy dictates, we stood and walked away from the distributor's desk to provide him with privacy. Upon rising we looked more closely at the thermometers. He wasn't keeping track of sales. He was plotting total precipitation, rain and snow, in northeastern Ohio, western Pennsylvania, and western upstate New York—an area some 350 miles northeast of his sales area in Indiana.

When we inquired as to his purpose, he stated, "That's where the headwaters of the Ohio River are formed. I know from these plots what to expect as flood stage in the late spring, and how many acres of farmland will be covered with water. When the flood waters recede they leave silt. My customers, the local farmers, know that good silt requires less fertilizer. So fertilizer sales go down as flood waters rise. However, that silt has to be treated, so fungicide, herbicide, and pesticide sales go up with flood water.

When we inquired as to how long he had been plotting flood stages, he replied, "Eighteen years." When we further inquired as to accuracy, he replied, "Right on." We took this information back to our client, a major producer of agrichemicals. It blew their minds. Today that manufacturer plots flood stages of major agricultural rivers worldwide, and the correlation to sales has proved invaluable.

Do the distributor's other suppliers participate in joint sales planning and forecasting? If so, what formats does the distributor favor?

7. What are the distributor's growth plans? What are the prospects for the next five years concerning current business?

Does the distributor believe that its current product mix is sufficient to meet the anticipated needs of the marketplace and the distributor's planned growth? How does the distributor perceive the role of your company and your products in his overall growth plan? Does the distributor have a business succession plan in the event of changes in management or ownership of his business?

In summary, all of the listed criteria are important in making the proper distributor selection decision for your market and products. The time, effort, and money that you expend in selecting the right distributor is a small investment compared to the untold costs of dealing with the wrong distributor and having to go through the termination and repeat selection process. Expediency in distributor selection is often more expensive than essential!

Either in person or by phone, hold screening interviews with prospective distributors to determine if they will meet your criteria and if they have an interest in selling your product line. It is useful to let the prospective distributors know that your call is a result of your survey of potential accounts.

Step 4. Hold Personal Interviews With Prospective Distributors

Preparation for the personal interview should include the following materials

- A copy of your annual report or, if privately held, any other documentation that describes your company, its past history, current financials, future growth plans, and market strategies
- A copy of your Statement of Distributor Policy
- The results of your survey of potential accounts
- A listing of the key accounts that you are interested in selling to in the distributor's market area
- A copy of your distributor sales agreement
- A profile of your current business (see Exhibit 5-1, Market Profile Analysis)
- A list of your current distributors
- Applicable product brochures
- Case histories and/or testimonials of successful sales relationships with current customers
- Product samples, if applicable

The interview should be conversational, with the intent of learning more about each other's total business, your expectations of a distributor, and the distributor's expectations of his suppliers. This interview should also delve into the culture of the distributor's market, product preferences, and local business mores.

Exhibit 5-1 is a Market Profile Analysis. This form is used to show the distributor a profile of your total business by identifying those vertical markets that represent your major sales volume, the number of potential customers in each vertical market segment, and your estimate of your total sales potential. This same form will be used later to give the distributor a referral base for developing a sales forecast with you.

In column 1, Industry/SIC, you list those key industries that, combined, represent 80 percent of your current business—

Exhibit 5-1. Market Profile Analysis.

COMPANY DATA

SIC/INDUSTRY	% TOTAL SALES	AVERAGE ANNUAL SALES/ACCOUNT ($000)	# POTEN ACCTS	EST. SALES POTEN. ($000)
3522 Farm Equip	19	248	78	19,344
3632 Hsld. Refrg	17	334	80	26,720
2259 Knit Mills	15	197	230	45,310
2819 Inorg Chem	15	194	100	19,400
3535 Conv. Equip	14	142	382	54,244
2221 Brdwvn Fab	12	213	216	46,008
2874 Phos Fert	8	158	312	49,296
TOTAL	100		1,398	260,322

DISTRIBUTOR DATA

$ TOT. SALES	AVERAGE ANNUAL SALES/ACCOUNT ($000)	# POTEN ACCTS	DIST. SALES POTEN.	EST. SHARE (%) ($000)	DIST. FCST. ($000)	EFF. RANK

your target markets. In column 2, Percent Total Sales, list the percentage of your total sales that each of these industries (vertical markets) represents. Column 3, Average Annual Sales/Account, requires you to calculate and list your average annual sales per a typical account in this industry.

Column 4, # Potential Accounts, is where you list how many potential accounts you have identified in this industry. This figure can be global, national, or regional depending upon your preference. And in column 5, Estimated Sales Potential, put the figure you get by multiplying column 4 by column 3.

Your "checklist" for this personal interview should include the following:

☐ *Credit and financial stability.* You have already requested financial and credit data from the prospective distributor. Now you must be in a position to share this same information as it concerns your company. What has been your past financial and sales performance? What are your goals and strategies for future growth, new markets, and new products?

☐ *Sales strength of the distributor.* Some of the questions you will seek answers to during this interview will involve your distributor selection criteria. The strength of the distributor's sales force depends on more than mere numbers of people. You will want to determine the ratio of inside to outside sales, and how the salespeople are assigned sales responsibilities. Are they assigned sales territories, specific accounts, specific markets?

You will want to determine what share of the market the distributor believes he holds against the local competition.

And, most important, what has been the rate of personnel turnover in the distributor's sales force? A high turnover rate indicates dissatisfaction among the distributor's sales personnel, so you must determine the reason behind a high turnover rate.

☐ *Sales competence.* You can't very well ask a distributor, "How competent is your sales force?" However, there are questions that may be asked that will give you an indication of how the distributor perceives the competence level of the sales force. For example:

— How knowledgeable are the sales personnel in terms of their product lines and suppliers?

— How often do they take advantage of supplier sponsored sales and product training programs?

— How successful are the sales personnel in prospecting for and establishing new business accounts?

— What type of compensation plan is used for the sales force and does it include special bonuses and/or incentives?

This last question concerning compensation may appear to be a strange way of determining competence, however our studies show that there is a direct relationship between perceived sales competence and compensation plans used by distributors. If we were to compare the knowledge required to be successful in a specific sales position versus the types of compensation plans used by distributors, we would find the following:

Level of Required Knowledge

Low: Visits accounts on a routine schedule, takes orders for catalogue items. *Type of Compensation:* Straight commission

Medium Low: Develops some depth into accounts, learns the key specifiers, determines customer needs, comfortable with longer term sales cycles. *Type of Compensation:* Salary plus commission

Medium: Develops long-term relationships within the account organization, attempts to sell as much of the product line as possible to match customer needs, develops contractual purchases. Good at prospecting and developing new accounts. *Type of Compensation:* Salary plus sales bonus

Medium High: Targets an accounts potential applications for the product line and develops a value-added need within the account organization. Develops single source

	agreements and can demonstrate contributions to the accounts profit. *Type of Compensation:* Salary plus profit bonus or profit share
High:	Works with accounts in management of inventory, JIT (just-in-time) deliveries, develops new product applications, initiates profit improvement strategies with accounts, negotiates long-term sourcing agreements, manages and trains other sales personnel. *Type of Compensation:* Salary plus equity

☐ *Market knowledge.* How well does the distributor and the distributor's sales staff understand the markets, and the potential accounts therein, to whom you wish to sell? Are they currently selling other products at these accounts? What is the depth of their relationship within these accounts?

☐ *Product mix.* Is the distributor's product mix complementary, supplementary, or directly competitive with yours? What is the breadth and depth of the distributor's product mix? If the product mix is too broad, your product may not receive the share of selling time you desire. If the distributor's product mix is too deep (too many products in the product line), the distributor may be experiencing inventory control or product turnover problems that could have a negative effect on the distributor's cash flow and corresponding ability to maintain your credit terms.

Does the distributor have "favorite" products or product lines that determine the positioning of the distributor's business? If so, are these products and/or product lines complementary to yours?

☐ *Sales performance.* What information is the distributor willing to share concerning past sales performance by product line? Does the distributor believe that the current product mix, based upon sales performance, is sufficient to meet current and anticipated market needs?

☐ *Growth.* How does the distributor perceive the growth potential of your products in the distributor's current market?

What are the distributor's long-term plans for continuance of business?

☐ *Sales forecasts.* How often does the distributor prepare sales forecasts, for what reasons, and what market indicators are important to the distributor? Does the distributor use any formal forecasting method?

If the distributor finances inventory through short-term bank financing, then you can be assured that the distributor is forecasting, or at least providing the bank with a prospectus, every time the inventory loan is refinanced.

☐ *Inventory handling capabilities.* Is the distributor equipped to handle your inventory requirements without additional capital investment? What does the distributor believe to be acceptable turnover of inventory and what inventory control programs does the distributor use? How does the distributor finance inventory?

☐ *Total facilities.* Does the distributor have sufficient facilities for storage, shipping, modification of products, or adding value as required by the market? Does the distributor have compatible communication facilities to correspond with you and to support the distributor's inside sales staff?

☐ *Management ability.* How does the distributor view the planning and training functions of management? What are the distributor's thoughts on cash management? Does the distributor control cash flow internally or does it use an outside accountancy or consultancy?

Are there well-developed lines of communication between the distributor and current suppliers? Who represent the distributor principals, board of directors, stockholders, and so on?

☐ *Succession.* What arrangements have been made to continue the distributor's business in the event of an involuntary change of the distributor management or ownership? Are the distributor's stockholders permitted to sell their shares to a third party?

You are now prepared to make your distributor selection. Don't be in a hurry! Examine all interview data, market data, and financial data against your selection criteria. If there are questions remaining, contact the distributor to gain clarification. Remember, this relationship with the distributor you are selecting is meant to be long term, and the distributor is to be integrated into your total sales and marketing strategy. Expediency is nice but seldom smart!

Upon making your decision, request another appointment with the selected distributor to negotiate your initial sales forecast, sales agreement, and initial inventory.

Write a personal thank-you letter to all distributors you have interviewed, compliment their businesses, inform them of your choice, and request that the communication lines you have established be kept open for future consultations. In other words, keep the contacts that you have established for future consideration.

Step 5. Negotiate the Initial Sales Forecast

Using the Market Profile Analysis (Exhibit 5-1), show the distributor the vertical market profile of your business. Then, using the left-hand side of the spreadsheet as a referral base, discuss with the distributor his anticipation of the vertical market profile for your products in his market area and estimate the percentages of each market as it will apply to the distributor's business.

Enter the distributor's estimate of sales percentage in column 6 under Distributor Data, Percent Total Sales. (See Exhibit 5-2 for an example of a completed Market Profile Analysis.)

You have shown the average sales or average annual sales to typical customers in each of these vertical markets. With the distributor, estimate the sales level the distributor can expect to attain at typical accounts in each of the distributor's vertical markets during the next three- to five-year period. The reason for discussing these figures in the long term, three-to-five years, is to set the distributor at ease. If the distributor believes that by answering this question he is making a commitment that could turn into a sales quota, he will be hesitant to cooperate with you. Enter the distributor's estimate in column 7, Average Annual Sales/Account.

Identify and agree upon the number of major potential accounts in each of the distributor's vertical markets. Enter the

Exhibit 5-2. Completed Market Profile Analysis.

COMPANY DATA | DISTRIBUTOR DATA

INDUSTRY/ SIC	% TOTAL SALES	AVERAGE ANNUAL SALES/ ACCOUNT ($000)	# POTEN ACCTS	EST. SALES POTEN ($000)	$ TOT. SALES	AVERAGE ANNUAL SALES/ ACCOUNT ($000)	# POTEN ACCTS	DIST. SALES POTEN. ($000)	EST. SHARE (%)	DIST. FCST. ($000)	EFF. RANK
3522 Farm Equip	19	248	78	19,344	10	90	8	720	25	180	6
3632 Hsld. Refrg	17	334	80	26,720	25	65	12	780	15	117	7
2259 Knit Mills	15	197	230	45,310	5	75	20	1,500	10	150	10
2819 Inorg Chem	15	194	100	19,400	20	100	6	600	33	198	5
3535 Conv. Equip	14	142	382	54,244	5	70	14	980	20	196	9
2221 Brdwvn Fab	12	213	216	46,008	15	50	16	800	20	160	8
2874 Phos Fert	8	158	312	49,296	5	60	10	600	25	150	4
TOTAL	100		1,398	260,322	85		86	5,980		1,151	

result in column 8, # Potential Accounts. Multiply this number by the distributor's estimate of average sales per account. That is, column 7 multiplied by column 8, with the result entered in column 9, Distributor's Sales Potential.

Next, agree with the distributor on what percentage of this potential—you and the distributor working together—can reasonably expect to achieve during the coming fiscal or calendar year. Enter this percentage in column 10, Estimated Share. Multiply the Distributor's Sales Potential, column 9, by this Estimated Share, column 10, to obtain the Distributor Forecast, column 11, for each vertical market.

Lastly, in the column marked, Effort Rank, jointly set priorities for your planned sales effort on each vertical market using the scale of 1 to 10, 10 being high.

You have now created a vertical market plan with the distributor while generating a sales forecast by vertical market. This is the first of the jointly developed plans you will be creating with the distributor. Three others—the Product Line Profit Analysis, the Tactical Sales Plan, and the Training Needs Analysis—will be discussed in later pages.

Step 6. Negotiating the Initial Distributor Inventory

At this point, many people who negotiate with distributors tend to get greedy. The distributor's initial inventory will make the order books look good. Forget it! *You are negotiating an investment, not an order.*

Salespeople negotiate orders; business executives negotiate investments. The distributor's initial inventory represents an investment in a business partnership that must be profitable to both parties. Find out how the distributor measures profit and what return on inventory investment he requires. Then, using the profit calculations from Chapter 2, compute the contribution margin and level of inventory turnover that is required to achieve the distributor's desired return on inventory investment.

For example, suppose in conversation with the distributor you learn that the distributor wants to "make 30 cents on the dollar" to remain profitable. Does that mean a 30 percent discount is required? No, it means that the distributor needs a return on inventory investment of 30 percent. Remember the formula from Chapter 2,

Contribution margin x inventory turns = ROII

Or the distributor may say, "I need a sales to inventory ratio of not less than 5 to 1." This means that the distributor is looking to achieve at least five inventory turns per year.

The distributor may say, "I need a 15 percent margin to break even." Does this mean a net on sales of 15 percent? No. It means that the distributor needs a 15 percent margin of safety (see Margin of Safety, Chapter 2).

Assuming the above, your negotiation of initial inventory must consider the following formulations:

ROII required (30 %) is expressed as 130 % or 1.30

Turnover required = 5

Break-even margin required = 15%

Contribution margin = ROII/turns = 130/5 = 26 percent

$$
\begin{aligned}
\text{Net profit (pre-tax profit)} \quad &= \quad \text{Break-even margin x contribution margin} \\
&= \quad 15 \text{ x } .26 \\
&= \quad 3.9 \text{ percent}
\end{aligned}
$$

From the above, calculate the optimum inventory to meet the distributor's profit parameters:

$$
\text{Optimum inventory} \quad = \quad \frac{(\text{Sales forecast x contribution margin})}{\text{ROII}}
$$

This means that initial inventory should not exceed .26/1.30, or 20 percent of the distributor's first year's annual forecast; 20 percent equals 5 turns.

Anything you can do to assist the distributor in maintaining lower levels of inventory or increasing inventory turns means a more profitable distributor. Your company's profitability may depend on minimum order requirements. That's fine; just make certain that your minimum order requirements are compatible with distributor inventory turns.

Step 7. Negotiate Your Distributor Sales Agreement

In Chapter 4 we provided a checklist of items to be negotiated in the sales agreement. We don't use the term *contract*. Even though your sales agreement is a legally binding contract, we prefer to think of it as a negotiated agreement between two independent business entities describing a cooperative sales and marketing effort.

Your legal department will, in all probability, want the distributor to sign a prepared thirty-page document of legal boiler plate. Don't fight it; however, convince your legal department that the following points are negotiable on an annual basis and should be treated as an attachment to the main body of the contractual boilerplate.

1. Define all parties to the agreement.
2. Negotiate and define the distributor's principal sales area, if in Europe, or primary area of responsibility, if in the United States, as that area where you will measure, evaluate, and support the distributor's sales performance.
3. Negotiate sales exceptions. Identify those customers and/or potential accounts that will be treated as direct sales accounts within the distributor's principal sales area. This does not prevent the distributor from selling to those accounts. It merely notifies the distributor that he will be competing with you for that business.
4. Negotiate and list the products that the distributor is expected to inventory and sell.
5. Negotiate training requirements and distributor participation therein.
6. Negotiate the initial levels of distributor inventory.

Step 8. Implement Your Distributor Identity Program

Often, we finish negotiations with a new distributor and believe that the job is complete. However, the next step is to inform the marketplace of the new alliance and to identify the distributor as your sales and marketing partner. On your company letterhead, signed by your highest sales executive or your company president, write a three- or four-paragraph letter introducing the new partnership. Make this letter available to the distributor for mailing to key potential customers or send it to a mailing list preferred by the distributor.

The mailing list should also include:

- Chambers of commerce within the distributor's market area.
- Business editors of news media in the distributor's market area.
- Your current distributors in the distributor's market area and distributors in abutting markets.
- Presidents or executive secretaries of civic organization chapters to which the distributor belongs—Rotary, Kiwanis, Exchange Club, etc.
- See that your own department heads and staff are also informed of the new distributor. There is nothing more embarrassing than having a newly appointed distributor call your office and receive the reaction, "Who are you?"

Within a reasonable amount of money, agree to pay 100% of the first advertisement or promotion which the distributor uses to introduce your company and your products to his market.

Offer to make some initial joint sales calls on major accounts which the distributor believes hold the greatest sales potential for the immediate future.

Step 9. Implement Your Initial Sales and Product Training Program

This is the critical test of your relationship with the new distributor. Up to this point, most of your discussions have been with distributor principals and management. You have been speaking of markets, market potential, support programs, inventory, and profit. But now you must face the distributor's sales force and, unknown to you, this is an adversarial relationship. "Management" has decided to take on a new product line, probably without consulting the sales force. And like all sales people, they have too much to do with the current distributor products. They don't like you!

You have five minutes to gain their hearts and minds!

Your initial presentation to the distributor's sales force must be:

1. Presented in their language
2. Concise, snappy, visual
3. Immediately usable by the distributor's sales force

The information you supply must be such that they can use it that day or the next day when talking to potential customers. It should include: a description of the product. What the product does and for what class of trade (customer profile). It should also emphasize the perceived benefits (why do they buy?).

Your training should be designed to address how the product is sold, not how to sell it. The distributor's salespeople know how to sell, but they don't know the selling process or sales cycle for effectively selling your product.

We have found that the following initial training format is well received and gains the support of the distributor's sales personnel.

1. Present a brief history of your company.
2. Present success stories detailing how the products have been successfully sold.
3. Describe the current market potential as it applies to the distributor's market area.

4. Describe the products benefits to current customers and why they both need and want the products.
5. Discuss, in detail, the sales support programs you are prepared to provide to the sales force.

These five points can be effectively presented in five minutes. The presentation can consist of one eighty-frame slide carousel and all eighty frames can be shown within these first five minutes.

Your job is to convince the salespeople that the products are easy to sell and profitable for both the sales force and the distributor. This first training program must be more market oriented than product oriented. If you attempt to get too technical or explain too much about the product, you will lose their interest, and the eventual support of the sales force.

Following the first five minutes, open the presentation to discussion and questions before to presenting any detailed information concerning product markets and product knowledge.

Teach the sales force how to read and use your product manuals, how to obtain answers to questions from potential customers, and how to penetrate potential customer accounts. Also, describe the various job functions in any potential customer organization likely to be involved in the decision to purchase your products.

Attempt to limit the total time for this first training session to ninety minutes, no more!

You may well be saying, "There's no way we can accomplish effective training in ninety minutes." Yes there is, because that's all the time you have for this first meeting. The attention span of the distributor's sales force, and their absorption level, will not permit more time. You can talk longer, but no one will be listening.

Prior to the training session, schedule three or four joint sales calls to be made with at least two of the distributor's sales personnel. Following the initial ninety-minute training session, spend the balance of the day making these sales calls. At the end of the business day, hold a second training session—of not more than one hour—when the involved salespeople critique the reception and interest shown by potential customers.

Schedule a follow-up training session within one month, and now take all the time you need. The attention span and absorption level will be there!

Remember, your function at this initial training session is to gain the confidence and friendship of the sales force.

Step 10. "Jointly," With the Distributor Sales Manager, Develop Your First Year Tactical Sales Plan

For most sales managers—and most sales people, for that matter—sales planning is onerous, cumbersome, and considered to be nothing more than helping the boss fill out his reports. Well, it's not that at all! Sales planning is critical to the success of any venture. However, it usually takes place at the executive level and, in many companies, is seldom communicated to the sales force.

The following is a format that we have used successfully with distributor sales forces to develop annual sales plans. It replaces the perception of onerous planning with a feeling of ownership. The format takes approximately forty-five minutes and at the end you have a tactical sales plan.

The Tactical Sales Plan

Planning consists of two basic activities: (1) development of strategies to attain the goal of the sales forecast; and (2) development of tactics to implement the strategies and evaluate the plan. The priorities developed using the Market Profile Analysis defined the vertical strategic markets where the sales forecast will be achieved. Now you must develop the strategic and tactical plans to penetrate each priority market.

1. In a meeting with the distributor's sales manager and/or members of the distributor's sales force, express every possible sales strategy that comes to mind for penetrating each priority market. Remember that a strategy says *what* you intend to do, it doesn't say *how* you intend to do it. Write and record every strategy mentioned. Don't attempt to evaluate what is

said, regardless of how inane it may sound. For instance, a strategy may be stated as, "concentrate sales efforts on the chemical-processing market," "develop new sales literature," "purchase a new delivery truck."

2. Use the letters *A, B,* and *C* to set priorities for each strategy mentioned. For example:

> *A* Important: The goal cannot be accomplished without implementing this strategy
>
> *B* Not important in and of itself, but may support an *A* strategy
>
> *C* Not important; forget it.

3. Reexamine each *A*-level strategy and set priorities, using numerals—1, 2, 3, etc.—to define the most important of the strategies. You may find that you have two *A*-1 strategies. Fine, merge them into one strategy.

4. On a separate sheet of paper, write your *A*-1 strategy.

5. Discuss the physical activities or tactics which you, the distributor personnel, and others must perform in order to implement the strategy. An example tactic may be something as simple as "Make an appointment" or "Prepare a product demonstration." Again, write and record everything that is said. Do not evaluate!

6. Using the letters *A, B, C* as above, set priorities for each tactic (activity) mentioned.

7. Start a Tactical Sales Plan (see Exhibit 5-3) for each strategy. Record all the tactics needed to achieve that strategy in the left-hand column, leaving some space between entries.

8. In the column marked Resource/Respon., negotiate and list the names of people in your organization, in the distributor's organization, and others—such as suppliers and customers—who will act as resources or have responsibility for performing each tactic.

9. Jointly, estimate and/or negotiate a time line or schedule for completion of each tactic. The Tactical Sales Plan indicates an annual schedule, listed as months 1–12. You may wish to alter this schedule to weeks, or even days.

Exhibit 5-3. Tactical Sales Plan.

GOAL: _____

STRATEGY: _____

TACTIC	RESOURCE/ RESPON.	01 02 03 04 05 06 07 08 09 10 11 12	CHECK POINTS	CONTINGENCY

10. Negotiate and agree upon the check points—either arbitrary dates or events which will be used to evaluate progress. At each check point, you have reason to be in communication with the distributor. If, let's say, you arrive at a check point and determine that a particular tactic isn't working, what are your contingency plans? If you look at your list of priorities, you will probably find that you have already established contingencies in some of your B priorities. At each check point you also have the opportunity to renegotiate the tactical plan, and it is suggested that you do so. The plan is not carved in stone, only the goal is.

Comments on the Tactical Sales Plan

The Tactical Sales Plan provides you with much more than a sales plan. It is a tool for evaluation of performance and should become an integral part of your sales agreement. Further, you have created a tool of communication within your organization. If a subordinate, superior, or member of another department is a resource for this plan, it gives the person a sense of ownership. Isn't it better if, say a project engineer is included in the plan, to have the project engineer know well in advance of your and the distributor's expectations, rather than to make a request of the engineer two weeks before you need the assistance?

With the Tactical Sales Plan you have accomplished something else very important. Wherever more than two persons are involved in a long-term commitment, there are going to be disagreements as to the purpose of the plan and each person's role. These potential disagreements are value clashes. Depending on internal values, the task, procedure, or plan will be viewed differently by people of differing values. But the Tactical Sales Plan holds appeal for many different values. It appeals to people who:

- Are pragmatic and goal oriented
- Desire management responsibility and seek an opportunity for recognition of accomplishment
- Seek a logical, systematic approach to task achievement
- Do not wish to take responsibility directly themselves but are willing to support others

- Seek acceptance as a team player but are not willing to be the team manager
- Prefer to take small steps toward goal accomplishment so as to minimize risks

All in all, the Tactical Sales Plan is one of your most useful management tools for dealing with distributors as well as with your own management team.

You have now completed the ten steps toward acquiring a new distributor. As we stated previously, implementation of these steps requires an average of six to eight weeks, plus substantial travel expense. But we know of no other procedure that is as effective.

Chapter 6

Implementing Distributor Pull-Through Programs

"Pull-through" is anything you do to pull business through the distributor sales channel. Advertising, local promotions, joint market and sales planning, joint inventory planning and control, joint sales calls, sales leads and referrals are all considered components of pull-through. Segmenting markets, products, and customers, and specifying that which is distributor business and that which is direct business, is another form of pull-through.

Market segmentation, as a stated policy, is a catalyst in the development of distributor loyalty. It tells distributors that you have a policy of supporting them rather than competing with them.

There still exists a school of thought, antiquated as it may be, that inventory is an incentive to sell, and the more a supplier can load up a distributor, the more incentive the distributor has to sell the supplier's products. This is called "push-through" and has no place in today's market. Push-through treats distributors as customers, wherein a distributor's purchase is considered a sale.

But there is no sale until the distributor sells the supplier's products! If you work for a boss who at the end of each month says, "Call the distributors and see how much [inventory] they can take," quit—before it's too late! You're working for someone who doesn't understand distributors and will probably destroy any possibility of building distributor loyalty.

Cooperative Advertising

Most distributors welcome the opportunity to participate in a well-planned cooperative advertising program, and most advertising agencies offer, and will administer, co-op programs for their clients.

A well-planned co-op program consists of the following elements:

1. The plan provides matching funds for advertising and sales promotion on a proportionately equal basis for all distributors. "Proportionately equal" means that your plan generates matching funds based on a formula that is the same for everyone. For instance, the distributor may earn $1 for each case of goods sold, or the distributor may earn 3 percent of net sales.

2. Distributor qualification for matching funds may be based on achieving a minimum threshold of sales. You may also place a cap on the maximum amount of funds to be earned.

3. Advertising copy and special promotions should be pre-approved by you, preferably in writing.

4. Advertising and promotional allowances should be paid to the distributor after the fact and only upon proof of payment for the advertisement or promotional expenditure.

5. You should have a written policy defining which advertising and promotional activities qualify for matching funds—that is, newspaper, trade journals, expositions, trade shows, training programs, and so on.

6. Advertising materials created by you or your advertising agency, for use by the distributors, should be pre-approved by a cross-section of your distributors.

Not many years ago, one of our clients developed an advertisement that depicted its trademark in the shape of an earth-moving plow—a bulldozer—pushing the trademark names of its competitors over the edge of a cliff. The distributors refused to use the materials or even allow their names to be mentioned in the advertisement. Why? Because the distributors also represented many of the competitive products depicted in the ad copy.

7. You should define the limitations and/or proper use of your logos and trademarks.

8. There should be stipulations as to how excess earned advertising funds are to be used, redistributed, or carried over at the end of each fiscal year.

9. National or global advertising is your responsibility and the distributors may not be back-charged for advertising that you create and place in national or global media.

10. More certain that all materials made available to the distributors are properly translated into the language and style of the distributor's market. Preferably, translations should be performed in the distributor's market area, by the distributor's advertising agency. Many languages are expressed in different local dialects and contexts, and what you may believe to be a proper translation may not be contextually correct for the distributor's market.

Local Promotions

Local promotions may take the form of point-of-sale materials, targeted advertising to specific market segments or class of trade, special presentation materials for local seminars, and emphasis on specific products within the product mix. Local promotions should be jointly planned—between you and the distributor—and budgeted within the co-op advertising budget. Too often, we have witnessed clients agreeing to a special advertising request from the distributor without defining the objective or desired result of the local promotion and/or assisting the distributor in planning the local promotion. This can be wasteful! On the reverse side, suppliers sometimes impose a local promotion on the distributor without the same joint planning and budgeting to ensure the promotion's success.

Point-of-Sale Materials

The following guidelines should apply to any point-of-sale materials developed by you or your distributor.

1. They should complement the distributor's total business as well as promote your products.
2. The materials should be designed for use over a specified time period. There is nothing that demeans a company's image more than antiquated signs, banners, and displays that have been in place too long and have become dust collectors.
3. Displays should be portable and easily assembled, and contain take-away pamphlets or brochures. You may think that the "portable and easily assembled" statement is redundant. However, we have seen some point-of-sale displays that require assembly by a construction engineer or someone who can spend a day erecting the display.
4. Displays should be designed to occupy a minimum of floor space or shelf space.
5. Displays should have a theme of interest to the distributor's market.

Targeted Advertising

Many distributors request that you assist them in developing advertising for specific market segments or for a specific class of trade in their markets. If you have identified the distributor's vertical market priorities (see Exhibit 1-1, the Target Market Profile), a program of product positioning for each vertical market should already be in place as part of your sales strategy.

If you have more than one distributor in a market, the targeted advertising may be somewhat difficult to administer as a co-op program. The initiating distributor may want specific mention in return for co-op payments, or may feel that the competitive distributor will be receiving free advertising. In this event, it is incumbent upon you to present an equitable co-op contribution program to each distributor or to administer the target advertising from other than a co-op budget.

Special Presentation Materials

You may be requested to work with a distributor to prepare special presentation materials for a planned in-house seminar or a distributor-sponsored open house. These requests should be honored and charged to the distributor within the stipulations of your co-op advertising budget. We suggest that you also make a company representative available to the distributor, to be present at any such seminar or open house.

Special Product Promotions

Special product promotions are usually viewed by the distributor as the responsibility of the supplier. Distributors see special product promotions as time-consuming and distracting from the distributor's total sales effort. Therefore, to gain the distributors cooperation, we suggest the following:

1. Administer special product promotions outside of the co-op advertising budget.
2. Design the special promotion to complement other distributor products that may be ancillary to yours.
3. Provide the distributor with a list of target markets or target customers for the special product promotion.
4. Offer a cash incentive to the distributor for product sales consummated during the special promotion.
5. Offer the assistance of a company sales representative to work with the distributor during the special promotion.

Trade Fairs, Shows, and Expositions

Trade fairs are an important aspect of doing business in world markets, especially in Europe. However, if you're like most sales executives, there's nothing you dislike more than standing on the concrete floor of a show booth for four or five days. Yet trade fairs are important, a major way to provide pull-through for your distributors.

To make your attendance at a trade fair less burdensome and more rewarding, we suggest the following:

1. Use your time to perform a competitive market analysis and market research.
2. Research how other companies—your competitors—are "positioning" themselves and their products.
3. Have a theme for your display that will highlight one or two specific products or product applications. Possibly the theme should highlight your company or your distributor network.
4. Have electronic order entry available to potential customers. Be able to enter orders via computer, directly from your show booth.
5. Invite potential customers to visit you at your booth.
6. Invite your local distributors to assist you in manning your booth and permit them to display their products and services that complement yours.
7. Publicize your attendance in trade journals, show journals, and personal letters to potential customers.
8. Screen all leads prior to imprinting and imprint only those who desire an immediate sales contact.
9. Retain conference space for business meetings with key potential accounts.
10. Use your time to identify other potential distributors/dealers.

All sales leads and orders generated at the trade fair should remain your property, and then be disbursed to the distributors only after the fair is over and you have had time to qualify each lead. If, conversely, the distributor is sponsoring the trade fair booth, then all sales leads and orders belong to the distributor.

One problem that arises in many countries is the import

duties charged on display products and materials. Even though the products are not being brought into the country for resale, you may still face customs and duty charges. For this reason, many companies compensate the distributor for supplying the necessary trade fair products and materials from distributor stocks.

One final and important point. Know the local law concerning alcoholic beverages at the trade fair. In Europe, it is expected that you will dispense alcoholic beverages. In the Middle East, such beverages are not permitted. In Singapore, you must have an authorized license. In the United States, it's not a good idea, for liability reasons.

Joint Sales Calls With Distributor Personnel

Successful joint sales calls are the ultimate in pull-through and can be provided to any distributor. However, few suppliers perform well on joint sales calls, and as a result many distributors discourage these calls. Where do you go wrong? Why shouldn't all distributors welcome your offers of joint sales calls?

The answer lies in the fact that most supplier salespersons feel superior to the distributor salesperson and, as a result, tend to preempt the distributor's salesperson in front of that person's customer. That's right, the distributor's customer! Too often supplier salespersons believe that the customers are theirs and that they have the superior knowledge to deal with customer requirements, complaints, and technical and product questions.

This may be true! And of course, the customer who purchases your product is, theoretically, yours. But your fault lies in the fact that supplier salespeople telegraph this message to the customer and, in so doing, subordinate the distributor's salesperson.

Your function, on a joint sales call, is to support, reinforce, and observe the distributor's salesperson—to observe in the sense of determining future training needs. You may say, "I've been on joint calls where I had no choice but to preempt because the distributor's salesperson couldn't answer the customer's question." That's fine, but there's a way of answering the customer without subordinating the distributor's salesperson.

Remember, there are two people making the sales call.

When you see that the distributor's salesperson may be unable to answer a customer's query, you might say something like, "That's an interesting question. *We* were talking about that this morning and this is what *we* believe." There are two people on the sales call. Keep the I out of the conversation. Of course, there will be times when you have no choice but to take over the sales call, but judge the situation first. If the call can be salvaged by a second call at a later date, then leave it be and use this call as an opportunity for training prior to the follow-up call.

Following are the basic rules for successful joint sales calls:

1. Know the purpose of the call and the role you are expected to play. Who will you be seeing? What questions are likely to be asked? What is the history of business relations between the distributor and this customer?
2. Remember that the customer belongs to the distributor.
3. Never refer to yourself. Always say *we*.
4. Never, never, never discuss price. Price is the distributor's prerogative.
5. Never preempt the distributor's salesperson.

Following any joint sales call, you should hold a critique with the distributor's salesperson. Psychologists tell us that performance critiques should be positive and reinforcing. That's easier said than done.

Let's assume that you have just completed a joint sales call that turned out to be a disaster. As you return to the car, the air is tense; there exists an unseen static. You know the call was bad, the distributor's salesperson knows the call was bad, and the distributor's salesperson knows that you know the call was bad. At this point, we have a rule: "He who speaks first, loses! So what do you do? The best way to dispel this tension is to use what we call the third-party referral. For instance, "That was an interesting call, Joe. When I was on a call with Mary last month we had a similar experience. Here's what we did. . . ." By using the third-party referral, you are not criticizing the salesperson; rather, you are letting the person know that he is not alone in having experienced a difficult sales call.

J. L. Beecroft, who was probably the dean of sales trainers

when he was with 3M, states that there are five ways in which we demotivate salespeople in a critique.

1. By telling them how they are doing
2. By continually manipulating them
3. By offering constructive criticism
4. By measuring activity rather than accomplishment
5. By making it appear that you don't believe they can succeed

We are all guilty of the above, and where distributor sales personnel are concerned, we are especially guilty of telegraphing item number 5.

If you believe that you are superior to the distributor's salespersons in terms of product knowledge and/or sales skills, it will become apparent in short order. Your job is to share this knowledge and skill with the distributor's salespersons, as a teacher and by example. However, in truth, not many supplier sales personnel have sales skills superior to distributor salespeople, but many believe they do.

When planning a joint-call itinerary, list those customers upon whom you wish to call and the purpose of the call, and forward this information to the distributor at least two weeks in advance. Also, leave time in your schedule to make calls at accounts where the distributor may desire your assistance.

When making joint sales calls outside of the United States, it is of course desirable to know the language of the country in which you are traveling; however, you will find that many businesspeople speak and understand English. During a joint sales call, don't be upset when the distributor's salesperson and the customer speak to each other in the native tongue. It is usually to clarify what you may have said. Be cautious about using slang expressions or making statements that could have dual meanings (double entendre).

Continuous Training

Training is also a form of pull-through. To be effective, training must be continuous and yield information that is immediately usable.

Formal training programs or seminars should be held with distributor personnel at least twice yearly, and informal training should be your goal each time you are with distributor personnel. Informal training comes from business discussions, answers to customer questions, discussions of real and hypothetical problem situations, and example.

Your training program agenda and content should be discussed with the distributor prior to your presentation, and should allow the distributor to modify or alter the training program to suit his priorities.

Don't presume to know what training the distributor personnel require. Design the training plan with the distributor, using the Training Needs Analysis form (see Exhibit 6-1). Ask the distributor's sales manager and/or the distributor principal to list the skills and disciplines required for sales success in their market, using the left-hand column of the Training Needs Analysis. Across the top of the other columns list the names of the distributor's salespeople.

Request the distributor to rate each salesperson as to how well he or she meets the criteria in the left-hand column, using a scale of 1 to 5, 5 being high. When each ranking is totaled horizontally, the distributor has drawn a profile of the strengths and weaknesses of the sales force as perceived by the distributor, not as perceived by you. The lower the horizontal grade, the more the distributor perceives a need for training.

All training should be more market oriented than product oriented. It should concentrate on how the market perceives, uses, and purchases your products. If your product is of a highly technical nature, the training should concentrate on what you know to be the most frequently asked questions by customers and how the distributor's salespeople can obtain direct technical assistance from you as required.

Effective training programs should incorporate the following guidelines:

Exhibit 6-1. Training Needs Analysis.

Skills and Disciplines	Salesperson's name					Total
Total						

1. Training program segments should not exceed ninety minutes.

2. Workbooks should be prepared in the language of the distributor and contain substantial space between paragraphs to allow the sales people to write notes and text.

3. Talk with the trainees, not to them! Invite participation by having some of the trainees relate stories to emphasize the training subject matter or to expand on a comment or an instruction you have presented. Visual aids preferred by most distributors; in order of preference, these are:

- 35mm slides
- Prepared flip charts
- VCR tapes of not more than thirty minutes duration
- Overhead transparencies

Use project sessions and simulated sales cases or studies wherever possible to reinforce subject matter.

Repeating what we have previously stated, the training must be immediately usable by the sales force. As one distributor stated to us, There's need-to-know and nice-to-know. Give my people the need-to-know!

Effective Communications

The complaint we hear most often from distributors concerns their difficulty in communicating with their suppliers and receiving prompt answers to their questions. In today's information age, there should be no valid reason for this situation.

Electronic communication, in its varied forms, is readily available in almost every major world market. Much of the information sought by distributors can be made available through e-mail, the Internet, electronic bulletin boards, or dedicated modems for privacy.

Copyrighted software, diskette programs, and coded access—which allow distributors to use their suppliers' data systems—should be used for:

- Order entry
- Order status inquiries

- Product pricing
- Technical reference libraries
- Competitive product comparisons
- Distribution and shipment tracking
- Electronic banking
- Fax transmission
- Video conferencing

You may think that these technologies are universally in place, but very few suppliers offer distributors access to these systems. Many suppliers think of their internal data systems as proprietary, and they are reluctant to open up their systems to outsiders.

Written communications are necessary whenever you want a permanent record of the communication, and should be used for changes in policies, product specifications, and pricing. Also, put reports of contacts with customers and/or potential customers in the distributor's market in writing, including personal and telephone contacts. Monthly or quarterly distributor performance reports should also be a part of your written communications.

Distributors also appreciate monthly or quarterly newsletters that describe success by other distributors in sales negotiations, sales promotions, and training programs.

In its newsletter, one of our clients requested that all distributors advise the company of excess or obsolete inventory. This inventory data were then published in the newsletter, so the distributors could buy and sell excess inventory among themselves. This policy reduced by approximately 50 percent the amount of returned goods from the distributors.

I often hear distributors complain that suppliers "never return calls." They say "It's impossible to get with anyone who can provide answers"; "The sales manager is always in meetings"; or "Their customer service people [inside sales, sales coordinators] don't know anything about our business." These are not insignificant gripes. Rather, they are serious problems that, if left unattended, can destroy a supplier-distributor relationship.

To be effective, you must provide a single point of contact for verbal communications with distributors. The people in this function should:

1. Be authorized to cut across organizational lines to obtain answers.
2. Be available at all times. You might consider having sales coordinators work staggered hours so that they are on duty when the distributor is working.
3. Have a working knowledge of the distributor's total business.
4. Keep the inside sales managers or field salespeople informed of all distributor contacts and requests.
5. Be organized and responsive. They must return all distributor phone calls within twenty-four hours. If they don't know the answer to a question, they should say so and state a precise time when the distributor can expect to have an answer.

The people who are assigned responsibility for sales coordination should have the opportunity to visit each distributor under their charge. And in a global operation, the sales coordinators should know the distributor's language.

All of what we have stated, in terms of establishing pull-through, may appear to be organizationally cumbersome and expensive. It is not! It is necessary if you have the true objective of integrating the distributor sales network into your total sales and marketing strategy. Well-designed and properly organized pull-through will result in increased sales, profits, market penetration, and loyalty. It will return your pull-through investments in short order, usually less than two years.

Chapter 7

Developing Distributor Loyalty and Your Fair Share of the Distributor's Sales Efforts

There are some sales executives who believe that they can demand share-of-time, based upon the sales volume share of the distributor's business, or that they can buy share-of-time through cleverly concocted incentive programs. Neither of these represent the management required to gain share-of-time.

Demanding share-of-time based upon your share of the distributor's total sales volume is a waste of time and makes it appear as though you are threatening the distributor with pulling your line unless you receive what you believe to be a fair share of the selling time. This is called management by intimidation and it doesn't work.

Incentive programs work to some extent, but we don't believe that incentive programs establish long-term motivation in the distributor's sales force. We believe that motivation is the product of two variables: desire and expectation.

People's desire to succeed is usually a given. If they don't succeed, it is because they don't have the expectation that they can succeed. They have constructed internal barriers, based upon their self-perception of the qualities of success.

Take, for example, a Little League baseball team. When those young players show up for the first day of team practice, they are motivated. They want to be on the winning team. But if the coaches don't work with them on the fundamentals of the game, offer encouragement, and build loyalty, the players become demotivated. Their desire to be a winner hasn't changed, but they no longer have the expectation that their team can win.

Most incentive programs are misdirected. They aim toward increasing a person's desire level, whereas the function of management is to build expectations. Therefore, when we speak of developing distributor loyalty and gaining a fair share of selling time, we must address the expectation levels of the distributors and their sales forces. We must attempt to channel these expectations into the desired level of success.

Nothing goes further to build expectations of success, loyalty, and cooperation than well-developed joint sales and market plans, profit plans, and inventory plans. Building expectations of success depends on the following key management disciplines.

Joint Sales and Market Planning

The key word here is *joint*. Market plans and sales plans, in the form of sales quotas, must be jointly developed with the distributor and take into consideration the individuality of the distributor's marketplace. Market plans at the corporate level are global in nature; market plans at the distributor level are individual and tailored to the distributor's market.

The jointly developed sales and marketing plans should be the primary criterion for evaluating distributor performance, and should be made an integral part of your distributor sales agreement when the agreement is renegotiated each year. These plans help to build distributor loyalty by identifying goals, showing the support that can be expected from you, and providing a tool for communication.

Joint planning provides an ancillary benefit. It gives the distributor a sense of ownership of your overall corporate marketing and sales goals. It also prevents personality clashes owing to miscommunication and spur-of-the-minute directives.

Joint planning makes arbitrary, financial, manufacturing, engineering, and other types of corporate-directed quotas obsolete.

Joint Profit Planning and Inventory Control

In any business relationship, it is essential that each party remain profitable and support the other in profit-improvement strategies and programs. Therefore, those companies that demonstrate a measurable concern for the profitability of their distributors are the ones that gain distributor loyalty.

The key to supporting distributor profitability is your support in the following areas:

1. Increased distributor sales measured by pull-through programs
2. Reduced distributor costs through pricing structure, return goods policies, economic order quantities, and co-op advertising
3. Reduced distributor costs through joint inventory-control planning to determine optimum inventory levels to support sales

We have already discussed items 1 and 2. So let's begin with item 3, inventory control.

You should monitor the distributor's inventory purchases on a continuous basis, and input the data in the Product Line Profit Analysis (see Exhibit 7-1), in the five columns on the Estimated Distributor Profit side of the page. But let's look at this handy form step by step.

The Products/Product Group is where you list the individual products or product groups that represent the distributor's

Exhibit 7-1. PRODUCT LINE PROFIT Analysis.

ESTIMATED DISTRIBOR PROFIT

PRODUCTS OR PRODUCT GROUP	ANNUAL PURCH. ($000)	TIMES ORD.-1	EST. CM MARGIN (.00)	CM. PROFIT ($000)
Terminals	50	4	.20	12.50
Monitors	35	6	.15	6.17
CPUs	28	3	.20	7.00
Modems	42	5	.25	1400
Operating	25	8	.20	6.25

PLANNED PROFIT

PLANNED PROFIT ($000)	ACTUAL MARGIN (.00)	PLAN ROII (1:X)	SALES REQD. ($000)	PLANNED INVENT. ($000)	TURNS REQ'D
15	.17	1.25	88.2	12.0	7.4
8	.18	1.25	44.5	6.4	7.0
10	.25	1.25	40.0	8.0	5.0
18	.17	1.25	82.4	11.2	7.4
8	.15	1.25	16.0	1.9	8.4

product purchases from you during the past year. The Annual Purchases column is where you list the distributor's annual dollar purchases for each product/product group. For the product turns (Times Ordered − 1), record the number of times the distributor purchased the products during the previous year and subtract 1. This represents your estimate of product turns. By subtracting 1 you are assuming that the distributor still has some inventory on hand.

In the Estimated Contribution Margin column, enter your estimate of the distributor's contribution margin percentage as equal to net sales minus the variable cost of sales expressed as a decimal. For the Contribution Margin (CM) Profit, enter your estimate of the distributor's contribution margin profit, expressed as dollars. For example:

(Purchases/1 − estimated margin) x estimated margin

From Exhibit 7-1, we can see that product group ABC is:

$$\frac{50}{(1 - .20) \times .20} = 12.50$$

Discuss the estimated profit data with the distributor and then say something stupid like, "Is this level of profit sufficient?" The answer is almost always no. Then use the Planned Profit section of the spreadsheet to create a plan for the distributor to achieve his profit goals with your product line.

For the planned profit, enter the planned or desired profit the distributor wishes to attain for each product or product group. In the Actual Margin column, enter the distributor's actual contribution margin as a percent (expressed as a decimal). For the Planned Return on Inventory Investment (ROII), enter the distributor's planned return on inventory investment. If the distributor wants a 25 percent return, that's a 125 percent return on inventory investment; expressed as a decimal, it is 1.25.

For the Sales Required column, calculate the sales required to obtain the desired profit as equal to the planned profit/actual contribution margin. To determine the planned inventory, calculate the optimum inventory to support sales and return the planned profit as equal to:

$$\frac{\text{Sales Required} \times \text{Contribution Margin}}{\text{ROII}}$$

Referring to Exhibit 7-1, you see that:

$$\frac{88.2 \times 17}{1.25} = \$12,000 \text{ Planned Inventory}$$

To figure the Turns Required, calculate the inventory turns as follows:

$$\frac{\text{Sales}}{\text{Planned Inventor}} = \text{Turns Required}$$

In Exhibit 7-1, this is:

$$\frac{88.2}{12.0} = 7.4$$

You have now developed a product-line profit plan for the distributor and, in the planned inventory column, a product-line sales forecast for yourself.

The Product Line Profit Analysis will be of help in monitoring the distributor profitability of your line and assist the distributor in becoming more profitable through improved inventory control. When examining Exhibit 7-1 you should ask, "What can I do to help the distributor improve his actual contribution margin?" Remember, the contribution margin is dependent on variable sales costs. Of course, the distributor would like you to reduce prices, but there are other ways you can influence this margin.

1. By helping to reduce sales cost through training, joint sales calls, advertising and promotion, and sales planning
2. By monitoring the distributor's ordering habits to ensure that he does not have too much inventory

Minimum Order Quantities

Beyond inventory planning, you should also develop minimum order quantities that are profitable to both you and the distributor.

Too often, minimum orders are decided by freight rates and shipping costs. For example, a seagoing container may be the least expensive way to ship, however this volume of goods may be uneconomic for distributors in terms of costs of possession. Shipping smaller quantities via air may be the most economic and profitable means overall. Choose your method of shipment only after considering all economic factors, not just freight rates. For instance, investigate time en route, ease and cost of entry into the distributor's country, pilferage and other risks involved when a shipment is not moving, and insurance and other delivery cost factors involved in getting your goods to the distributor.

Your minimum order quantity should be calculated as your cost of order processing (not including the cost of goods) divided by your planned contribution margin.

Customer Communication

In many countries, direct contact with the manufacturer or supplier of branded products is an essential component of doing business. Your distributors will often request your presence on joint sales calls, trade fairs, and the like in order to give credibility to themselves as well as to your company. This is especially true when developing markets, as most distributors do not spend a lot of time doing missionary work. (Missionary work involves developing new account potential outside of the distributor's current account base.)

Potential customers, when visiting your country, often request a personal visit to your office or factory. You may also receive phone calls or faxes directly from the distributor's customers. In each instance of a direct contact with a distributor's customer, you should advise the distributor of the context of the contact and any actions required by either yourself or the distributor. There is nothing more embarrassing than for a distrib-

utor to learn secondhand of a policy or specification change negotiated between you and one of the distributor's customers.

In markets where you have more than one distributor, all
distributors should be notified of direct customer contacts. We
find that a standard call report, in the format of Exhibit 7-2,
faxed to a distributor or distributors enhances communication
and builds distributor loyalty.

Executive Visits

Distributors and their customers appreciate visits by those in
your company who have executive status. Discussions between
executives at the same functional level provide exceptional
pull-through and credibility for both you and the distributor.
One word of caution, however. If one of your nonsales executives is planning to visit a customer or a distributor, train the
person first. Let him or her know what can and cannot be discussed. Make the person aware of the current status and past
history of your relations with the distributor and the distributor's customers. And do not allow the visiting executive to
imply or say, "My door's always open, call me anytime." That
comment has done more to destroy distributor relations and
distributor loyalty than any other single action. It also destroys
the lines of communication you have worked so hard to establish by encouraging the distributor to bypass them.

Sales Referrals and Sales Leads

All sales leads received by you should be qualified by you prior
to forwarding them to a distributor. Where you have more than
one distributor in a market, each should receive the sales lead.

Sales referrals for pending orders should be handled in the
same manner. However, if you believe it is more efficient, and
will reduce conflict between the distributors, you may want to
have a referral policy that we refer to as the rollover policy,
wherein each distributor is given referrals in turn. In the event
of a direct contact for a sales referral, where the potential customer asks for a recommendation of a specific distributor, it is

Exhibit 7-2. Report of customer contact.

DATE: _____ .

CUSTOMER NAME: _____ .

COMPANY NAME: _____ .

PHONE: _____ .   FAX _____ .

REASON FOR CONTACT:

RESULTS OF DISCUSSION AND ACTION REQUIRED:

CONTACT INITIATED BY:

best to advise the customer of all distributors who could handle the order and let the customer make the selection.

Profit Monitoring and Analysis

Your contribution to the profitability of the distributor and to your company can be measured and evaluated in ways other than the inventory control and profit-planning procedures.

For example, consider the elements of profit measurement, net sales, cost of sales, contribution margin, operating profit, margin of safety, and ROII. Ask yourself, "How can I positively influence each of these elements for my distributors?"

Sales

Your potential for influence in the realm of sales should be obvious. How can you measure your direct and indirect participation in the distributor's sales volume? The answer lies in your efforts in joint sales calls, training, market, sales and profit planning, advertising, and promotion programs.

Cost of Goods Sold

You have very little direct effect on the cost of goods, since it is a function of your finance and accounting departments, market demands, and competitive pricing. However, you do have an indirect influence on the cost of goods through your planning efforts with your distributors.

Because the product-line forecasts generated by the inventory plan, which allows your company to take advantage of the economies of scale in the purchase of raw materials, machinery utilization, warehousing, and distribution, you can offer the lowest possible prices to your distributors. Inventory planning also allows the distributor to reduce cost of goods by maximizing product turnover and taking advantage of economic order quantities and shipping quantities.

One factor that is often overlooked in the cost-of-goods equation is the total pipeline cost. Pipeline costs are those invisible costs of time involved in the delivery of goods that you technically own until you receive payment for the goods.

Exhibit 7-3 represents a compilation of these costs in terms of days on hand, or in terms of the time in which your money is tied up in the cost of manufacturing, warehousing, shipping, and waiting for payment. In Exhibit 7-3, all costs are based on the annual costs of possession from Exhibit 3-2, or 28 percent.

An examination of pipeline costs shows domestic costs in which the customer requires that inventory not exceed three days. Your total delivery time to the distributor is five days, and the distributor's delivery time to the customer is one day. The six-day delivery time equals 0.46 percent of the cost of the goods being shipped. If you are shipping to a distributor in a world market and total delivery time to the customer is now thirty days, the pipeline cost soars to 2.30 percent of the cost of goods being shipped. Thus, anything that you and the distributor can do to reduce time in the pipeline will increase profitability for both of you.

Selling and Administrative Costs

Your contribution to selling and administrative cost reduction is measurable within your company and, more importantly, as a contribution to your distributor's profitability. In essence, any effort you make to generate sales to the distributor's market increases his revenue without increasing his sales costs. For instance, you contribute to the distributor's profitability through:

- Joint sales calls that reduce the distributor's sales cycle and increase sales
- Joint sales and market planning to define and develop priorities concerning key markets and key potential accounts
- Working with the distributor to coordinate the effective use of advertising, sales promotion, trade fairs
- Training of the distributor's sales force and measuring your training effectiveness
- Coordination of communication between the distributor and your company personnel

Exhibit 7-3. Pipeline costs.

	Days	Costs As % Of Sales Revenue
MANUFACTURING CYCLE TIME		
Procurement	60	4.60
Processing	30	2.30
Delivery	5	0.38
DISTRIBUTOR HANDLING TIME		
Receiving	1	0.08
Warehousing	1	0.08
Order processing	2	0.15
Delivery	1	0.08
CUSTOMER REQUIREMENTS		
Receiving	1	0.08
Days, inventory required	3	0.23
DISTRIBUTOR INVENTORY REQUIRED	14	1.07
MANUFACTURER'S INVENTORY REQUIRED	21	1.61
RECEIVABLES OUTSTANDING	45	3.45
ANNUAL COST of POSSESSION		28.00
TOTAL PIPELINE COSTS		14.12

Contribution Margin

A small increase in the distributor's contribution margin can result in a more substantial increase in the distributor's margin of safety. Remember that the contribution margin is the net sales minus the cost of goods minus the variable selling costs. Consider the comparison in Exhibit 7-4, in which the impact of a mere 1 percent improvement in the distributor's contribution margin leads to a 3.3 percent increase in margin of safety and a 17 percent reduction in break-even sales volume.

You might think that your distributor will never share that kind of information with you. However, if you begin by showing your preliminary operating data to the distributor, the distributor will likely cooperate in kind.

Exhibit 7-4. Percentage contribution to distributor's profitability.

	Distributor Operating Data	Your Profit Contribution	Total To Distributor
Net sales	100%	0%	100%
Cost of goods sold	65%	0%	65%
Other variable selling expenses	8%	(−) 1%	7%
Contribution margin	27%		28%
Fixed costs	25%	0%	25%
Pre-Tax profit	2%		3%
Margin of safety	7.40%		10.71%
Breakeven volume*	363%		346%

*Breakeven volume determines the amount of sales needed to offset total costs and maintain the required contribution margin.

Evaluation of Distributor Performance

Fair and constructive performance appraisals are another major contributor to increased distributor loyalty. At this point, we have discussed three documents—part of your sales agreement—that will be used for performance evaluation. All three documents have been jointly negotiated with the distributor and signify the distributor's concurrence.

The Market Profile Analysis (Exhibit 5-2) defined vertical market priorities and showed current market share in the Average Sales/Account column. The Tactical Sales Plan (Exhibit 5-3) described the responsibilities of each party in attaining mutually agreed upon sales goals. The Product Line Profit Analysis (Exhibit 7-1) defined product line inventory, sales, and product turnover plans. There is one other document used to evaluate and compare distributor performance, for which the distributor had no negotiated input. It's called the Workload Analysis (Exhibit 7-5 and Exhibit 7-6).

The Workload Analysis is a statistical, visual aid that allows you to compare the relative standing of your distributors, based upon their performance to forecast. The analysis is accomplished in five columns, as follows:

First column: Distributor's name
Second column: The distributor's annual sales forecast
                    for your products
Third column: The distributor's percentage of the total
                    forecast of the distributor sales network
Fourth column: The distributor's actual sales volume
Fifth column: The distributor's actual sales divided by
                    the distributor's percentage of the total
                    forecast (column 4/1% of column 2). For
                    example, for Distributor L in Exhibit 7-5:

$$\frac{\$310,000}{\$2,500} \; = \; \$124,000$$

The graph shown in Exhibit 7-5 is a computer compilation obtained by sorting column 5 in descending order and establishing a median sales/1 percent of forecast number. The graph indicates that distributor L has the highest sales per each 1 percent of

Exhibit 7-5. Workload Analysis spreadsheet.

Company Forecast $_____   10,000,000

Distributor Name	Distributor Sales Forecast	Distributor % of Forecast	Distributor Sales	Distributor Sales/1% of Sales Forecast
L	$250,000	2.50%	$310,000	$124,000
D	$800,000	8.00%	$880,000	$110,000
C	$1,050,000	10.50%	$1,150,000	$109,524
F	$620,000	6.20%	$650,000	$104,839
G	$1,500,000	15.00%	$1,470,000	$98,000
MED'N				$93,893
K	$1,750,000	17.50%	$1,600,000	$91,429
B	$720,000	7.20%	$650,000	$90,278
H	$970,000	9.70%	$820,000	$84,536
J	$680,000	6.80%	$550,000	$80,882
A	$380,000	3.80%	$290,000	$76,316
E	$450,000	4.50%	$240,000	$53,333
TOTAL	$9,170,000	91.70%	$8,610,000	
AVERAGE	$833,636	8.34%	$782,727	$93,893

Exhibit 7-6. Workload Analysis chart.

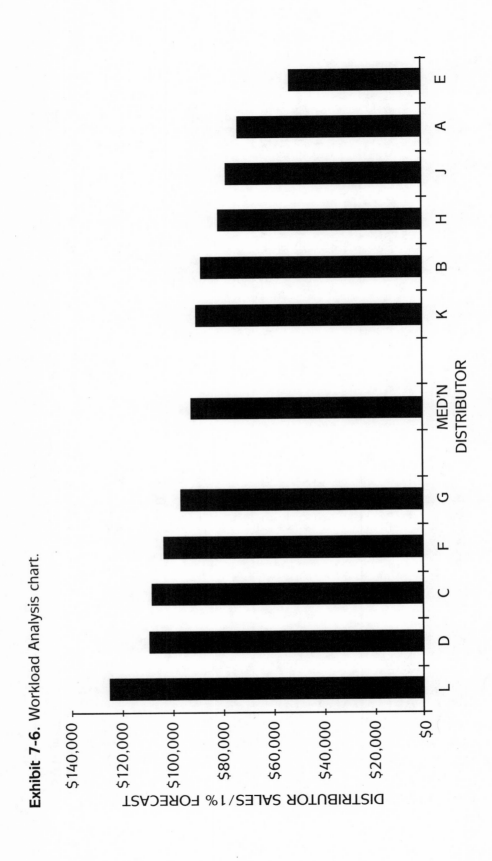

forecast, while distributor E has the lowest sales per 1 percent of forecast ratio. Does this mean that distributor L has shown superior performance compared to E? No, it indicates that you have to investigate the disparity and determine why it exists.

Distributor L may have under-forecast, may have many large accounts, may have a very compact sales area, may have better trained sales personnel, or may have fewer product lines. Distributor E, on the other hand, may have over-forecast, may have many small accounts, may have a widely dispersed sales area, may have the need for additional sales training, or may have many product lines.

The Workload Analysis is an indicator of performance, not an evaluator. It is an excellent tool for initiating discussions with those distributors who are widely separated from the performance median. We have found that most distributors like to know their standing as compared to your other distributors, and that it tends to be a motivator rather than a demotivator.

Incentive Compensation Programs

Most incentive programs proposed to distributors by their suppliers are an unwelcome burden. The distributors tell us that incentive programs are seldom equitable within their sales force, demand administrative time, and don't accomplish their intention of securing long-term motivation and achievement by the distributor's sales force.

There is one program, however, that has been in existence since 1923 that is welcomed by many distributors and does achieve long-term results. It's a profit rebate program established by Alfred G. Sloan, then president of General Motors.

For the program to work, the supplier needs to track the contribution to profits made by each distributor. You know the distributor's monthly sales figures and should know your variable costs of supporting each distributor. Sales minus variable costs equals the distributor's contribution to your contribution margin profit. Thus, the company agrees, at the beginning of its fiscal year, to set aside a percentage of excess contribution margin profit, generated by the distributors, for redistribution to the distributors at year end. (See Exhibit 7-7.)

Exhibit 7-7. Profit rebate table.

Month	1	2	3	4	5	6	7	8	9	10	11	12
SALES FORECAST (cum.)	100	200	300	400	500	600	700	800	900	1000	1100	1200
ACTUAL SALES (cum.)	150	225	300	460	540	680	800	950	1100	1250	1400	1600
MINIMUM ACCEPTABLE CONTRIBUTION MARGIN %	0.35	0.35	0.35	0.35	0.35	0.35	0.35	0.35	0.35	0.35	0.35	0.35
PROFIT PLAN	35	70	105	140	175	210	245	280	315	350	385	420
ACTUAL PROFIT	52.5	78.75	105	161	189	238	280	332.5	385	437.5	490	560
REDISTRIBUTION PROFIT												42

Exhibit 7-8. Profit plan rebate chart.

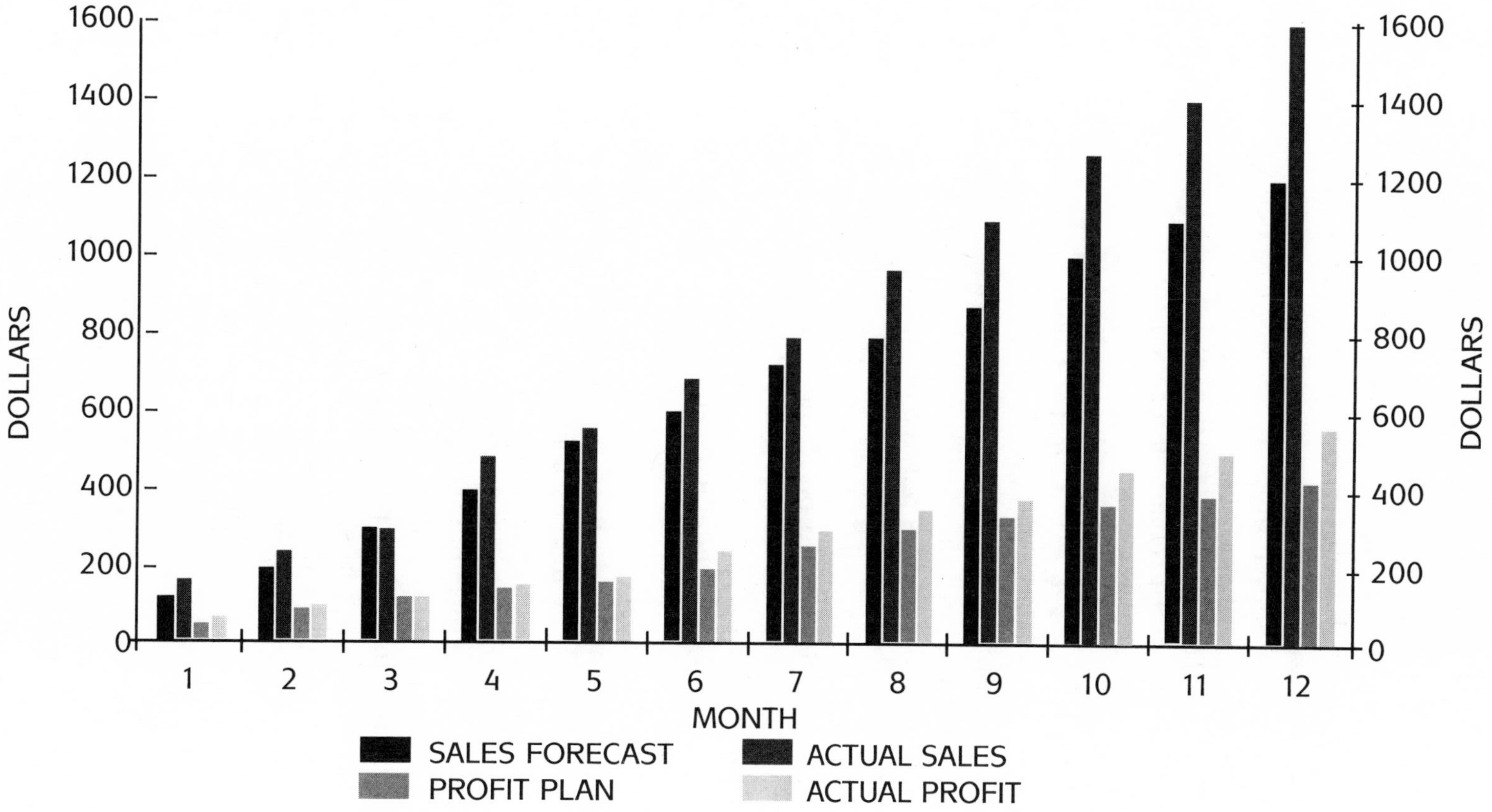

Each tenth of a percent above the minimum acceptable contribution margin—your profit plan—is then calculated as worth a fixed monetary amount. For example, consider a distributor whose forecast of $1.2 million was exceeded by $400,000, for a total sales volume of $1.6 million. According to the program, you have set a minimum acceptable contribution margin—in the example shown in Exhibit 7-8—of 35 percent. The distributor's total profit contribution was $560,000, versus a profit plan of $420,000 or an excess profit to the company of $140,000. If the company's profit rebate plan called for a 30 percent redistribution of excess profits, then this distributor would have received a payment of $42,000 at the end of the fiscal year.

You may say, "What if the distributor intentionally underforecasts at the beginning of the year in order to earn more rebate money?" Remember, the forecast was developed jointly between you and the distributor!

Some companies pay rebates quarterly instead of annually, believing that this does more to provide distributor incentive. This plan is the basis for automobile dealers earning rebates, which can be passed on to the consumer. Although one dealer may earn a rebate and its competitor for the same model of automobile may not, there is no price discrimination because the plan is equally available to all of the company's dealers and is earned.

In summary, any form of joint planning and inclusion of the distributor into your total sales and marketing efforts will be rewarded by increased loyalty and share of time.

Incentive programs should be based upon rewarding distributor performance and should be equitably measurable by you and the distributor.

Do not implement incentive programs which affect the price the distributor pays for your goods such as incentive discounts. When you start playing around with incentive pricing you create price differentials which are difficult to administer and legally justify.

Chapter 8
Distributor Advisory Councils

Spending time with distributors to communicate your interest in them as an integral component of your sales and marketing strategy is very effective when you have the time.

Unfortunately, building and maintaining distributor relationships is extremely time-consuming. One person cannot effectively manage more than ten distributors at a time, with six being the ideal. So what do you do if you have a worldwide network that includes hundreds of distributors? How can you possibly communicate well with all of them?

The answer can be to establish a distributor advisory council—a group of your distributors who work together to advise you about their market needs, product acceptance, desirable product improvements, competition for your products, and policy alterations required to meet changing legal and business environments.

The council may have a world focus or be a regional one; generally, regional councils are preferable. Regional councils work well because the markets within the region share a common business culture. It is easier for them to communicate with each other and to agree on business conditions in their regional markets.

Appropriate regions for councils are Asia or the Pacific, Europe, Western and Central Europe, Latin America, NAFTA countries, and the Middle East. The countries that appear to be independent of market regions are Japan, India, the Union of South Africa, the developing economies of the former Soviet Union and the emerging economies of Africa.

Invitation and Selection of Council Members

All distributors should be invited to become council members via a personal letter (see sample letter, Exhibit 8-1) describing the function of the council, the meeting format, and the expected benefits to the distributors and your company.

From all distributors responding positively to the invitation for council membership, select a cross-section representing large and small distributors from different geographic and cultural markets. Make the number of participants divisible by 3. For instance six, nine, twelve, or fifteen distributors (nine and twelve have historically been the most workable numbers), with the intent that one-third will be appointed to the council for a one-year term, one-third will be appointed for a two-year term, and one-third will be appointed to serve a three-year term. That way you'll establish a rotating council membership in which at the end of each year the one-third of the members will be replaced. All distributors appointed to the council after the first year will serve three-year terms.

Organizational Considerations

The councils should meet with you at least twice per year. The first meeting should be an organizational one to develop the council's agenda. The second meeting should be for you to report back on and discuss your company's progress in addressing the points set forth in the council's agenda. The third meeting should be on or near the anniversary of the first meeting, at which time a final report can be made by the company concerning all agenda items from the previous year. Also, a new agenda can be set for the coming year.

The first meeting of the council is critical. If not properly organized, it can rapidly degenerate into an unproductive grievance session. Use a facilitator who is unknown to the dis

Exhibit 8-1. Letter to distributors.

Dear _____:

    You are invited to become a member of our proposed Distributor Advisory Council.

    We believe that we can be of better service to our distributors through an active discussion of your needs and your consultations concerning the requirements of your markets.

    The purpose of the Council will be to advise us of your support requirements, the perceived product and service needs of your market, competitive situations in your market, and the needs of our other distributors with whom you are familiar.

    The Council will consist of nine of our distributors who will be requested to serve terms on the Council as follows:

- Three distributors will be appointed to serve a term of one year.
- Three distributors will be appointed to serve a term of two years.
- Three distributors will be appointed to serve a term of three years.

    At the end of the first year, three additional distributors will be appointed to serve a three-year term, therein establishing a rotating Council in which three different distributors will be appointed each year.

    You will be requested to attend at least two meetings each year. The first meeting will be to establish an agenda of topics you wish to discuss with us and a presentation of your concerns to us. The second meeting, to be held within six months of the first meeting, will be our report to you of recommended solutions and progress being made in addressing your other concerns where we have not yet devised solutions.

    We will reimburse all of your expenses for Council meeting attendance and participation.

    Please advise us of your willingness to serve on the Council and of any concerns you may wish to discuss.

Sincerely,

tributors to help them set an agenda to be discussed with company personnel.

The first step is for each council member to recite all topics of concern. The facilitator needs to be sure that all concerns are listed, regardless of how trivial they sound. Then have the council members discuss each topic and agree upon a priority rating: *A*, *B*, and *C*, according to the following criteria:

A Important: The topic is of primary concern to a majority of the council members. *Example:* Poor product quality.

B Potentially important: Not important in and of itself, but a topic that could grow into an *A* priority if not addressed. *Example:* Dissatisfaction with training formats.

C Not important: Forget it. *Example:* A council member's complaint about his country's policy on inflation.

It has been our experience that council members compile a list of thirty to forty concerns. Of these, about fifteen are *A* priorities. List each *A* priority topic on the Report Card (see Exhibit 8-2) and request that each member further set his own priorities by placing an *X* in the upper half of the box in the column that signifies his priority from 5 to 1 (5 being high). Next, request that the members give the company a grade, or ranking, in the lower half of the box in the column, indicating the company's performance regarding the distributor's priority.

Compile the distributors' priorities and the company's rankings and compute an average for each. Any topics for which the difference between distributor priorities and company ranking exceeds 0.5 becomes a critical topic for discussion. The facilitator will then prepare an agenda for discussion with company personnel, and advise the council that the discussion will be limited to those critical items, and that further discussions may ensue concerning all other *A*-rank priorities.

The facilitator will next request the council to elect from among themselves a council chair and a recording secretary.

Following the meeting of the council, which usually consumes a half-day, the council then meets with company executives. The company will appoint a liaison person to work with the council on each critical topic and promise to report a solu-

Exhibit 8-2. Report Card.

KEY:

| Distributor Priority/ |
| Company Rating |

< PRIORITY/RATING >

Discussion Item:	5	4	3	2	1	TOTAL
Quality of Part 15674						
Competition from XYZ Co.						
Packaging of Parts						
Technical Manual Update						

tion and/or progress within six months or at the next council meeting.

Reporting and Communication

Following each council meeting, a condensed version of the minutes including the results of the Report Card is forwarded to all distributors in the region. Also, each distributor is sent a copy of the Report Card, with only the A-ranked priorities filled in. At this point, you should ask the distributors to fill out their own priority rankings and assessments of the company's handling of each concern.

Earlier we advised against sending distributors questionnaires. This is not a questionnaire. It is an opportunity for all of the distributors to express their concerns to the council. The returns from this mailing will surprise you, as they tend to run approximately 80 percent of those solicited. Typically, the results will vary less than 0.1 plus or minus from the council's compilation of priorities.

Management of the Advisory Council

The person charged with coordinating council activities, developing future agendas, and providing liaison oversight should be the highest ranking sales executive in the company.

The distributors' expenses for travel to and from meeting sites, lodging, and meals should be reimbursed by the company. Because you are providing the distributors with an opportunity to meet as competitors, in some instances it may also be desirable for the company to have legal counsel at each.

If you follow the above organizational and management guidelines, you can create a proactive and cooperative distributor advisory council. Consider the following success stories.

- The Ameritech Council, with company editorial approval, publishes a quarterly newsletter advising all distributors of items of interest generated via communications between the council and the company.

- The Carrier Corporation's distributor council was instrumental in designing the training program that Carrier uses worldwide to train heating, ventilating, and air-conditioning service personnel.
- The Scott Paper Company's UK council assisted in the development and management of a two-tier distribution system.

The success of well-organized and managed distributor advisory councils in assisting company managements, and in devising distributor-dealer support programs, are well documented.

Epilogue

What we have provided in this book is a guide to developing and managing your distributor sales channels in most world markets. We have offered you a pragmatic, step-by-step approach to become a more effective manager of worldwide distributors, beginning with the basic knowledge required and carrying through to the management techniques to be successful.

There is much more to be learned as new world markets develop with each passing year. For example, at the present time, not much information is available concerning the distributor channels that will have to be created in the emerging markets of the former Soviet States, China, most of Africa, Central America, and the consolidated South American markets under Mercosur and the Andean Pact.

The laws of individual countries regarding distributors are becoming less restrictive as the marketplace dictates more openness and greater flow and diversification of products. Although many governments still attempt to protect their home industries, the flow of goods into world distributor channels is increasing at an almost exponential rate.

Instabilities in world currency markets are still a major concern for most companies. However, the U.S. dollar, the Deutschemark, the British pound, and the Japanese yen are the world's currencies of choice. Secondary stable currencies include the dollars of Canada, Singapore, Hong Kong, and Australia; the Argentine peso; the French, Swiss, and Belgian franc; the Dutch guilder; and the Swedish krona.

Banking is becoming more international, and foreign credits and other financial instruments of trade are being aggressively marketed by the more progressive world banks. The United States is far behind the rest of the world when it comes to international banking. However, we anticipate that current banking reforms before the Congress (1995) will allow U.S. banks to become competitive on a world basis.

Managers of many U.S. companies are beginning to learn about world marketing, but they have a long way to go to match the competitive capabilities of most Europeans, Japanese, and Southeast Asians. The unwillingness, or possibly the inability, of U.S. managers to spend the time required to learn about the culture of a foreign country—and at least a modicum of its language—is startling. This situation must change rapidly in U.S. businesses and in the offerings of the U.S. business schools.

Currently, next to Canada, Europe is the largest market for U.S. goods and services, followed by Southeast Asia. Tomorrow's markets will slowly begin to include the rest of the world, beginning with the neglected South American markets, the enigmatic China market, the mysterious markets of India and much of the Middle East, the provincial markets of Japan, and the cloistered markets of Eastern Europe. And although the development may be three decades away, the markets of black Africa will also emerge as a primary player in world trade.

Politics will always be with us, however we see a growing trend away from political provincialism, as witnessed by the growing number of regional free-trade alliances and the recent ratification of GATT by the U.S. Congress. In the United States, Europe, Japan, and China, politics still holds tremendous sway over business, but eventually the politicians will have to heed Mr. Gorbachev's words.

We are firm believers that there will eventually be no such thing as a domestic economy. We will have only a world economy, of which each company must be an integral player and competitor. This will require the development of new management strategies and philosophies and, in many instances, the development and management of strong and effective, well-trained and profitable, distributor sales networks!

Appendix A

Laws Affecting Distributor Relations

UNITED STATES

Sherman Anti-Trust Act: Sections 1–3

Section 1. Every contract combination in the form of trust or otherwise, or conspiracy, in restraint of trade or commerce among the several States, or with foreign nations, is declared to be illegal. Every person who shall make any contract or engage in any combination or conspiracy declared by these sections of this title to be illegal shall be deemed guilty of a felony, and, on conviction thereof, shall be punished by a fine not exceeding one million dollars if a corporation or, if any other person, one hundred thousand dollars or by imprisonment not exceeding three years, or by both said punishments, in the direction of the court.
[2 July 1890, chap. 647, sec. 1, 26 Stat. 209, as amended, 15 U.S.C.A. sec. 1 (Supp. I 1975)]

Section 2. Every person who shall monopolize, or attempt to monopolize, or combine or conspire with any other person or persons, to monopolize any part of the trade or commerce among the several States, or with foreign nations, shall be deemed guilty of a felony, and, on conviction thereof, shall be punished by a fine not exceeding one million dollars if a corporation or, if any person, one hundred thousand dollars or by imprisonment not exceeding three years, or by both said punishments, at the discretion of the court. [2 July 1890, chap. 647, sec. 2, 26 Stat. 209, as amended, 15 U.S.C.A. sec. 2 (Supp. I 1975)]

Section 3. Every contract, combination in form of trust or otherwise, or conspiracy, in restraint of trade or commerce in any Territory of the United States or District of Columbia, or in restraint of trade or commerce between any such Territory and another, or between any such Territory or Territories and any State or States or the District of Columbia, or with foreign nations, is declared illegal. Every person who shall make any such contract or engage in any such combination or conspiracy, shall be deemed guilty of a felony, and, on conviction thereof, shall be punished by a fine not exceeding one million dollars if a corporation or, if any other person, one hundred thousand dollars or by imprisonment not exceeding three years, or by both said punishments, in the discretion of the court. [2 July 1890, chap. 647, sec. 3, 26 Stat. 209, as amended, 15 U.S.C.A. sec. 3 (Supp. I 1975)]

Clayton Act: Sections 2 & 3, as amended
The Robinson-Patman Act

Section 2a. That it shall be unlawful for any person engaged in commerce, in the course of such commerce, either directly or indirectly, to discriminate in price between different purchasers of commodities of like grade and quality, where either or any of the purchases involved in such discrimination are in commerce, where such commodities are sold for use, consumption, or resale within the United States or any Territory thereof or the District of Columbia or any insular possession or other place under the jurisdiction of the United States, and where the effect of such discrimination may be substantially to lessen competition or tend to create a monopoly in any line of commerce, or to injure, destroy, or prevent competition with any person who either grants or knowingly receives the benefit of such discrimination, or with customers of either of them: *Provided*, that nothing herein contained shall prevent differentials which make only due allowance for differences in the cost manufacture,* sale, or delivery resulting from the differing methods or quantities in which such commodities are to such purchasers sold or delivered: *Provided, however*, That the Federal Trade Commission may, after due investigation and hearing to all interested parties, fix and establish quantity limits, and revise the same as it finds necessary, as to particular commodities or classes of commodities, where it finds that available purchasers in greater quantities are so few as to render differentials on account thereof unjustly discriminatory or promotive of monopoly in any line of commerce; and the foregoing shall then not be construed to permit differentials based on differences in quantities greater than those so fixed and established: *And provided further*, That nothing herein contained shall prevent persons engaged in selling goods, wares, or merchandise in commerce from selecting their own customers in bona fide transactions and not in restraint of trade: *And provided further,* That nothing herein contained shall prevent price changes from time to time where in response to changing conditions affecting the market for or the marketability of the goods concerned, such as but not limited to actual or limited deterioration of perishable goods, obsolescence of seasonal goods, distress sales under court process, or sales in good faith in discontinuance of business of the goods concerned. [19 June 1936, chap. 592, sec. 1, 49 Stat. 1526, as amended, 15 U.S.C. sec. 13.]

Section 2b. Upon proof being made, at any hearing on a complaint under this section, that there has been a discrimination in price or services or facilities furnished, the burden of rebutting the prima-facie case thus made by showing justification shall be upon the person charged with a violation of this section, and unless justification shall be affirmatively shown, the Commission is authorized to issue an order terminating the discrimination: *Provided, however,* That nothing herein contained shall prevent a seller rebutting the prima-facie case thus made by showing that his lower price or the furnishing of services or facilities to any purchaser or purchasers was made in good faith to meet an equally low price of a competitor, or the services or facilities furnished by a competitor. [19 June 1936, chap. 592, sec. 1, 49 Stat. 1526, as amended, 15 U.S.C. sec. 13]

Section 2c. That it shall be unlawful for any person engaged in commerce, in the course of such commerce, to pay or grant, or to receive or accept, anything of value as a commission, brokerage or other compensation, or any discount in lieu thereof, except for services rendered in connection with the sale or purchase of goods, wares, or merchandise, either to the other party to such transaction or to an agent, representative, or other intermediary therein where such intermediary is acting in fact for or in behalf, or is subject to the direct or indirect control to

---

* Author's note: Even though the law states that manufacturing cost justification may be used to justify a price differential, the courts have historically, since 1936, held that manufacturing cost justification be disallowed because the higher-volume, long-run manufacturing costs reduction is being subsidized by those who pay full price on shorter manufacturing runs.

any party to such transaction other than the person by whom such compensation is so granted or paid. [19 June 1936, chap. 592, sec. 1, 49 Stat. 1526, as amended, 15 U.S.C. sec. 13]

Section 2d. That it shall be unlawful for any person engaged in commerce to pay or contract for the payment of anything of value to or for the benefit of a customer of such person in the course of such commerce as compensation or in consideration for any services or facilities furnished by or through such customer in connection with the processing, handling, sale, or offering for sale of any products or commodities manufactured, sold, or offered for sale by such person, unless such payment or consideration is available on proportionally equal terms to all other customers competing in the distribution of such products or commodities. [19 June 1936, chap. 592, sec. 1, 49 Stat. 1526, as amended, 15 U.S.C. sec. 13.]

Section 2e. That it shall be unlawful for any person to discriminate in favor of one purchaser against another purchaser or purchasers of a commodity bought for resale, with or without processing, by contracting to furnish or furnishing, or by contributing to the furnishing of, any services or facilities connected with the processing, handling, sale, or offering for sale of such commodity so purchased, upon terms not accorded to all purchasers on proportionally equal terms. [19 June 1936, chap. 592, sec. 1, 49 Stat. 1526, as amended, U.S.C. sec. 13]

Section 2f. That it shall be unlawful for any person engaged in commerce, in the course of such commerce, knowingly to induce or receive a discrimination in price which is prohibited by this section. [19 June 1936, chap. 592, sec. 1, 49 Stat. 1526, as amended, U.S.C. sec. 13]

Section 3. It shall be unlawful for any person engaged in commerce, in the course of such commerce, to be a party to, or assist in, any transaction of sale, or contract to sell, which discriminates to his knowledge against competitors of the purchaser, in that, any discount, rebate, allowance, or advertising service charge is granted to the purchaser over and above any discount, rebate, allowance, or advertising service charge available at the time of such transaction to said competitors in respect of a sale of goods of like grade, quality, and quantity; to sell, or contract to sell, goods in any part of the United States at prices lower than those exacted by said person elsewhere in the United States for the purpose of destroying competition, or eliminating a competitor in such part of the United States; or, to sell, or contract to sell, goods at unreasonably low prices for the purpose of destroying competition or eliminating a competitor.

Any person violating any of the provisions of this section shall, upon conviction thereof, be fined not more than $5,000 or imprisoned not more than one year, or both. [19 June 1936, chap. 592, sec. 3, 49 Stat. 1528, as amended, 15 U.S.C. sec 13a.]

Federal Trade Commission Act Section 5 (a)(1) (15 U.S.C.A. Section 45)

Section 5(a)(1). Unfair methods of competition in or affecting commerce, and unfair or deceptive acts or practices in or affecting commerce, are declared unlawful. [26 September 1914, chap. 311, sec. 5, 38 Stat. 719, as amended, 15 U.S.C.A. sec. 45 (Supp. I 1975)]

OTHER NATIONS*

ALGERIA

Sales agreements must be registered. Applicable law: Law #78-02, 1978, as modified, 1988, 1990.

ARGENTINA

Anti-trust. Applicable law: Law #22,262, 1980. Criminal Code: Law #22,802.

Advertising. Disallows the negative use of a competitor's trade name or logo; re: Pepsi Challenge, 10/94.

AUSTRIA

Termination of agents or distributors. Applicable law: Trade Agents Act, 1993, para. 25.

BAHRAIN

Termination of agents or distributors. Applicable law: Amiri Decree #23, 1975, as amended by Legislative Decree #10, 1992, and arts. 164–174 and 194–203 of the Law of Commerce, Amiri Decree #7, 1987.

Registration of sales agreements is required under the above laws.

BELGIUM

Termination of agents or distributors. Applicable law: Unilateral Termination of Indefinite Exclusive Agreements, Law of 7/27/61 and Law of 4/13/71 and 4/21/71.

---

*Author's note: This compilation of country laws is printed with the permission of Baker & McKenzie.

BRAZIL

Anti-trust. Applicable law: Law #8,884, 6/11/94.

Termination of automotive vehicle distributors. Applicable law: Law #6,729, 11/28/79, as amended by Law #8,132, 12/26/90.

Termination of independent agents. Applicable law: Law #4,886, 12/10/65, as amended by, Law #8,420, 5/8/92.

COLOMBIA

Termination of agents or distributors. Applicable law: Commercial Code, arts. 1317–1331.

COSTA RICA

Termination of agents or distributors. Applicable law: Law #6209, 3/9/78, as amended by Executive Decree #8599, 5/5/78 and Decree #13519-S, 4/19/82.

CYPRUS

Termination of agents. Applicable law: Laws of Cyprus, sec. 161–170, chap. 149.

DOMINICAN REPUBLIC

Termination of agents or distributors. Applicable law: Law #173, 4/6/66, as amended by Law #263, 12/31/71, Law #622, 12/28/73 and Law #664, 1977.

ECUADOR

Termination of agents or distributors. Applicable law: Supreme Decree 1038-A, Official Register #245, 12/31/76.

EL SALVADOR

Termination of agents or distributors. Applicable law: Commercial Code, arts. 392–410 and 1066–1097, as amended by Decree #247 and Decree #237, 12/23/85.

FINLAND

Termination of agents. Applicable law: Law #417, 5/8/92.

FRANCE

Termination of agents or distributors. Applicable law: Decree #58-1345, 12/23/58, as amended by Law #91-153, 6/21/91.

GERMANY

Termination of agents or distributors. Applicable law: Commercial Code, sec. 89.

GREECE

Termination of agents. Applicable law: Commercial Code, arts. 90–94; Civil Code, arts. 211–215; Law 307/76, as amended by Presidential Decrees 407/87 and 219/91.

GUATEMALA

Termination of agents or distributors. Applicable law: Decree #78-71, 8/25/71, Official Gazette, 10/1/71.

HONDURAS

Termination of agents or distributors. Applicable law: Decree #459, 11/24/77, as amended by Decree #804, 9/10/79.

INDONESIA

Termination of agents or distributors. Applicable law: Civil Code, art. 1266.

Registration of sales agreements. Applicable law: Ministry of Industry Decree #135/Kp/VI/91, 6/3/91.

IRAQ

Termination of agents or distributors. Applicable law: Supreme Decree 1038-A, Official Register #245, 12/31/76.

ISRAEL

Termination of agents. Applicable law: Agency Law of 1965.

ITALY

Termination of agents or distributors. Applicable law: Civil Code, arts. 1742–1752, as amended by Law #204, 5/3/85 and Legislative Decree #303, 9/10/91.

JAPAN

Registration of sales agreements. Applicable law: Japan Fair Trade Commission, all agreement of more than one year duration and any agreement which contains resale price restrictions.

JORDAN

Termination of agents or distributors. Applicable law: Art. 864, Civil Code, Law #43, 1976; Art. 18, Law #44, 1985, art. 97, Commercial Code, Law #12, 1966.

Registration of sales agreements is required under the above laws.

KUWAIT

Termination of agents or distributors. Applicable law: Law #36, 1964; Law #37, 1964; Decree #68, 1980.

Registration of sales agreements is required under the above laws.

LEBANON

Termination of agents or distributors. Applicable law: Decree #34, 1967, as amended by Decree #9639, 1975.

Registration of sales agreements is required under the above laws.

LIBYA

Termination of agents or distributors. Applicable law: Registration of Agreements; Law #33, 1971, and implementing regulations in Decree #40, 1971; Law #87, 1975 and implementing regulations in Decree #73, 1975.

MYANMAR

Nationalization of Enterprises Law, 1962, only the government may be a distributor.

NETHERLANDS

Termination of agents. Applicable law: Commercial Code, Book I, Title 4, arts. 74–74S, as amended, 7/5/89.

NICARAGUA

Termination of agents or distributors. Applicable law: Decree #13, 12/22/79 modifying Decree #287, 2/2/72.

NORWAY

Termination of agents. Applicable law: Commercial Agent Act, 6/19/92. Termination of distributors. Applicable law: Law of June 1916, as amended by, Law of June 1, 1973.

OMAN

Termination of agents or distributors. Applicable law: Royal Decree #26, 1977, Ministerial Order #11, 1985.

Registration of sales agreements is required under the above laws.

PAKISTAN

Termination of agents or distributors. Applicable law: Contract Act, 1872, sec. 205.

PARAGUAY

Termination of agents or distributors. Applicable law: Decree Law #7, 3/27/91, as amended by Decree Law #194, 7/6/93.

PHILIPPINES

Termination of agents or distributors. Applicable law: Presidential Law #1789.

PORTUGAL

Termination of agents or distributors. Applicable law: Decree Law #176/86, 7/3/86.

PUERTO RICO

Termination of agents. Applicable law: Law #75, 6/24/64, as amended by 10 L.P.R.A., sec. 278, 1984; Law #21, 12/5/90.

QATAR

Termination of agents or distributors. Applicable law: Law #3, 1985, as amended by Law #10, 1989 and Law #4, 1986.

Registration of sales agreements are required by the above laws.

RUSSIA

Termination of agents or distributors. Applicable law: Civil Code, 1964 and Principles of Civil Legislation, 1991.

SAUDI ARABIA

Termination of agents or distributors. Applicable law: Royal Decree M/11, 1962, as amended by Royal Decree M/5, 1969, M/8, 1973, and M/32, 1980 and implementing regulations in Ministerial Decision #1897, 1981.

SOUTH KOREA

Registration of sales agreements. Applicable law: Art. #24 of the Anti-Monopoly and Fair Trade Law, 1991 and Art. #28 of the implementing Enforcement Decree and Economic Planning Board Notice #50, 10/1/87.

SPAIN

Termination of agents. Applicable law: Law 12/1992 and Royal Decree 1438, 8/1/85.

SWEDEN

Termination of agents. Applicable law: Law #351, 1991.

SWITZERLAND

Termination of agents. Applicable law: Law of Agency, 2/4/49, and art. 418a, Swiss Code of Obligations.

TANZANIA

Termination of agents or distributors. Applicable law: Law of Contract Ordinance, 1961.

THAILAND

Termination of agents or distributors. Applicable law: Civil and Commercial Code, sec. 827.

TURKEY

Termination of agents. Applicable law: Turkish Commercial Code, Book I, chap. VIII, arts. 116–134.

UNITED ARAB EMIRATES

Registration of sales agreements. Applicable law: Federal Law #18, 1981, as amended by Federal Law #14, 1988 and Ministerial Resolution #47, 1989.

VENEZUELA

Anti-trust; price fixing. Applicable law, arts. 10.1 and 10.2, Venezuela Anti-Trust Law.

Intellectual property. Trademarks and patents are NOT protected after two years of non-use. Applicable law: Resolution #914, 3/29/61, Official Gazette, 5/10/61.

Foreign debt. Applicable law: Resolution #46, 11/10/94: Official Gazette, 11/11/94; Foreign debt may not be incurred in commerce without the prior approval of the Minister of Finance.

Appendix B
List of Formulas

Contribution Margin

$$\text{Contribution margin} = \text{Net sales} - \text{cost of goods sold} - \text{variable selling costs}$$

Inventory Turns Required

$$\text{Turns required} = \frac{\text{Sales}}{\text{Planned inventory}}$$

Margin of Safety

$$\text{Margin of safety} = \frac{\text{Pre-tax profit}}{\text{Contribution margin}}$$

Minumum Selling Price

$$\text{Minimum selling price} = \frac{\text{Actual costs}}{1 - \text{industry average contribution margin}}$$

Net Profit

$$\text{Net profit} = \text{Break-even margin} \times \text{contribution margin}$$

Operating Profit

$$\text{Operating profit} = \text{Contribution margin} - \text{fixed cost}$$

Optimum Inventory

$$\text{Optimum inventory} = \frac{\text{Sales forecast} \times \text{planned contribution margin}}{\text{Planned ROII}}$$

Pre-Tax Profit

$$\text{Pre-tax profit} = \text{Operating profit} - \text{depreciation} - \text{current maturing long-term debt} - \text{other charges against profit}$$

Ratio Between Contribution Margin and ROII

$$\text{Contribution margin required} = \frac{\text{ROII}}{\text{Est. turns}}$$

Return–on–Inventory–Investment (ROII)

$$\text{ROI} = \frac{\text{Net sales}}{\text{total cost of inventory}}$$

$$\text{ROII} = \text{Contribution margin} \times \text{inventory turns}$$

Appendix C
Blank Forms

Target Market Profile

	CUSTOMER LIST					INDUSTRY LIST			
(1) Customer Name	(2) Industry: SIC Code	(3) Annual Sales To. ($000)	(4) Size Factor (#EMP)	(5) Sales:Emp. ($)	(6) Industry: SIC Code	(7) Sales:Emp. ($)	(8) Total Employment	(9) Est. Sales Poten. ($000)
TOTAL								

Target Market Profile

CUSTOMER LIST

INDUSTRY LIST

(1) Customer Name	(2) Industry· SIC Code	(3) Annual Sales To· ($000)	(4) Size Factor (#EMP)	(5) Sales·Emp. ($)	(6) Industry· SIC Code	(7) Sales·Emp. ($)	(8) Total Employment	(9) Est. Sales Poten. ($000)
TOTAL								

Target Market Profile

CUSTOMER LIST

INDUSTRY LIST

(1) Customer Name	(2) Industry/ SIC Code	(3) Annual Sales To: ($000)	(4) Size Factor (#EMP)	(5) Sales/Emp. ($)	(6) Industry/ SIC Code	(7) Sales/Emp. ($)	(8) Total Employment	(9) Est. Sales Poten. ($000)
TOTAL								

Profit Calculations

Operating Income Data	Currency	%
NET SALES	_____	_____
Variable costs of sales		
Cost of goods sold	_____	
Direct sales expenses	_____	
Materials	_____	
Warehousing and handling	_____	
Freight in	_____	
Delivery	_____	
SUBTOTAL	_____	_____
CONTRIBUTION MARGIN (net sales − variable costs)	══════	══════
Allocated fixed costs		
Salaries	_____	
Benefits	_____	
Insurance	_____	
Prepaid taxes	_____	
SUBTOTAL	_____	_____
OPERATING PROFIT (contibution margin − allocated fixed costs)	══════	══════
Depreciation	_____	
Current maturing; LT debt	_____	
Other	_____	
SUBTOTAL	_____	_____
PRE-TAX PROFIT (operating profit − depreciation − current maturing − other costs)	══════	══════
MARGIN OF SAFETY		_____
RETURN ON INVENTORY INVESTMENT		_____

Profit Calculations

Operating Income Data	Currency	%
NET SALES	————	————
Variable costs of sales		
Cost of goods sold	————	
Direct sales expenses	————	
Materials	————	
Warehousing and handling	————	
Freight in	————	
Delivery	————	
SUBTOTAL	————	————
CONTRIBUTION MARGIN	════	════
(net sales − variable costs)		
Allocated fixed costs		
Salaries	————	
Benefits	————	
Insurance	————	
Prepaid taxes	————	
SUBTOTAL	————	————
OPERATING PROFIT	════	════
(contibution margin − allocated fixed costs)		
Depreciation	————	
Current maturing; LT debt	————	
Other	————	
SUBTOTAL	————	————
PRE-TAX PROFIT	════	════
(operating profit − depreciation − current maturing − other costs)		
MARGIN OF SAFETY		————
RETURN ON INVENTORY INVESTMENT		————

Profit Calculations

Operating Income Data	Currency	%
NET SALES	_____	_____
Variable costs of sales		
Cost of goods sold	_____	
Direct sales expenses	_____	
Materials	_____	
Warehousing and handling	_____	
Freight in	_____	
Delivery	_____	
SUBTOTAL	_____	_____
CONTRIBUTION MARGIN (net sales – variable costs)	══════	══════
Allocated fixed costs		
Salaries	_____	
Benefits	_____	
Insurance	_____	
Prepaid taxes	_____	
SUBTOTAL	_____	_____
OPERATING PROFIT (contibution margin – allocated fixed costs)	══════	══════
Depreciation	_____	
Current maturing; LT debt	_____	
Other	_____	
SUBTOTAL	_____	_____
PRE-TAX PROFIT (operating profit – depreciation – current maturing – other costs)	══════	══════
MARGIN OF SAFETY		_____
RETURN ON INVENTORY INVESTMENT		_____

Variable Costs Audit, Annual Costs

Cost of inventory possession	____ %	sales
Inquiry & quotation processing	____ %	sales
Order entry processing	____ %	sales
Invoice processing	____ %	sales
Sales accounting	____ %	sales
Advertising & sales promotion	____ %	sales
Incremental direct sales staff support	____ %	sales
Other variable costs	____ %	sales
Total	____ %	sales

Variable Costs Audit, Annual Costs

Cost of inventory possession	_____ %	sales
Inquiry & quotation processing	_____ %	sales
Order entry processing	_____ %	sales
Invoice processing	_____ %	sales
Sales accounting	_____ %	sales
Advertising & sales promotion	_____ %	sales
Incremental direct sales staff support	_____ %	sales
Other variable costs	_____ %	sales
Total	_____ %	sales

Variable Costs Audit, Annual Costs

Cost of inventory possession	_____ % sales
Inquiry & quotation processing	_____ % sales
Order entry processing	_____ % sales
Invoice processing	_____ % sales
Sales accounting	_____ % sales
Advertising & sales promotion	_____ % sales
Incremental direct sales staff support	_____ % sales
Other variable costs _____	_____ % sales
Total	_____ % sales

Cost of Entry Worksheet

MARKET RESEARCH

Fees paid
(market research consultants,
ad agencies, etc.) $_____

Directories & publications $_____

Software
(market research data) $_____

TRAVEL

Market identification
(requiring physical presence
in the market) $_____

Survey of potential accounts
(requiring physical presence
in the market) $_____

Distributor interviews $_____

Distributor selection $_____

DISTRIBUTOR START-UP

Distributor identity program
(mailers, signage, brochures,
catalogs, etc.) $_____

Sales and market planning $_____

Sales & product training $_____

Initial inventory costs $_____

Initial advertising & promotion $_____

OTHER INCREMENTAL COSTS $_____

TOTAL $_____

Cost of Entry Worksheet

MARKET RESEARCH

Fees paid
(market research consultants,
ad agencies, etc.) $_____

Directories & publications $_____

Software
(market research data) $_____

TRAVEL

Market identification
(requiring physical presence
in the market) $_____

Survey of potential accounts
(requiring physical presence
in the market) $_____

Distributor interviews $_____

Distributor selection $_____

DISTRIBUTOR START-UP

Distributor identity program
(mailers, signage, brochures,
catalogs, etc.) $_____

Sales and market planning $_____

Sales & product training $_____

Initial inventory costs $_____

Initial advertising & promotion $_____

OTHER INCREMENTAL COSTS $_____

TOTAL $_____

Cost of Entry Worksheet

MARKET RESEARCH

Fees paid
(market research consultants,
ad agencies, etc.) $_____

Directories & publications $_____

Software
(market research data) $_____

TRAVEL

Market identification
(requiring physical presence
in the market) $_____

Survey of potential accounts
(requiring physical presence
in the market) $_____

Distributor interviews $_____

Distributor selection $_____

DISTRIBUTOR START-UP

Distributor identity program
(mailers, signage, brochures,
catalogs, etc.) $_____

Sales and market planning $_____

Sales & product training $_____

Initial inventory costs $_____

Initial advertising & promotion $_____

OTHER INCREMENTAL COSTS $_____

TOTAL $_____

Annual Cost of Inventory Possession Worksheet

Current commercial interest rate	11%
Current money market rates available	<u>7%</u>
Lost investment opportunity (11% – 7%)	4%
True cost of money (11% + 4%)	15%
Warehousing and handling costs (percent of sales)	7%
Insurance and taxes on inventory (percent of sales)	4%
Cost of outstanding receivables (percent of sales)	2%

TOTAL ANNUAL COST OF POSSESSION:

15% + 7% + 4% + 2% = 28%

Annual Cost of Inventory Possession Worksheet

Current commercial interest rate	11%
Current money market rates available	<u>7%</u>
Lost investment opportunity (11% – 7%)	4%
True cost of money (11% + 4%)	15%
Warehousing and handling costs (percent of sales)	7%
Insurance and taxes on inventory (percent of sales)	4%
Cost of outstanding receivables (percent of sales)	2%

TOTAL ANNUAL COST OF POSSESSION:

15% + 7% + 4% + 2% = 28%

Annual Cost of Inventory Possession Worksheet

Current commercial interest rate	11%
Current money market rates available	<u>7%</u>
Lost investment opportunity (11% – 7%)	4%
True cost of money (11% + 4%)	15%
Warehousing and handling costs (percent of sales)	7%
Insurance and taxes on inventory (percent of sales)	4%
Cost of outstanding receivables (percent of sales)	2%

TOTAL ANNUAL COST OF POSSESSION:

$$15\% + 7\% + 4\% + 2\% = 28\%$$

Market Profile Analysis

COMPANY DATA

SIC/INDUSTRY	% TOTAL SALES	AVERAGE ANNUAL SALES/ ACCOUNT ($000)	# POTEN ACCTS	EST. SALES POTEN. ($000)

DISTRIBUTOR DATA

$ TOT. SALES	AVERAGE ANNUAL SALES/ ACCOUNT ($000)	# POTEN ACCTS	DIST. SALES POTEN.	EST. SHARE (%) ($000)	DIST. FCST. ($000)	EFF. RANK

Market Profile Analysis

COMPANY DATA

SIC/INDUSTRY	% TOTAL SALES	AVERAGE ANNUAL SALES/ ACCOUNT ($000)	# POTEN ACCTS	EST. SALES POTEN. ($000)

DISTRIBUTOR DATA

$ TOT. SALES	AVERAGE ANNUAL SALES/ ACCOUNT ($000)	# POTEN ACCTS	DIST. SALES POTEN.	EST. SHARE (%) ($000)	DIST. FCST. ($000)	EFF. RANK

Market Profile Analysis

COMPANY DATA

DISTRIBUTOR DATA

SIC/INDUSTRY	% TOTAL SALES	AVERAGE ANNUAL SALES/ ACCOUNT ($000)	# POTEN ACCTS	EST. SALES POTEN. ($000)	$ TOT. SALES	AVERAGE ANNUAL SALES/ ACCOUNT ($000)	# POTEN ACCTS	DIST. SALES POTEN.	EST. SHARE (%) ($000)	DIST. FCST. ($000)	EFF. RANK

Tactical Sales Plan

GOAL: _____

STRATEGY: _____

TACTIC	RESOURCE/ RESPON.	01 02 03 04 05 06 07 08 09 10 11 12	CHECK POINTS	CONTINGENCY

Tactical Sales Plan

GOAL: _____

STRATEGY: _____

TACTIC	RESOURCE/ RESPON.	01 02 03 04 05 06 07 08 09 10 11 12	CHECK POINTS	CONTINGENCY

Tactical Sales Plan

GOAL: _____

STRATEGY: _____

TACTIC	RESOURCE/ RESPON.	01 02 03 04 05 06 07 08 09 10 11 12	CHECK POINTS	CONTINGENCY

Training Needs Analysis

Skills and Disciplines / Salesperson's name						Total
Total						

Training Needs Analysis

Skills and Disciplines / Salesperson's name						Total
Total						

Training Needs Analysis

Skills and Disciplines / Salesperson's name						Total
Total						

Product Line Profit Analysis

ESTIMATED DISTRIBOR PROFIT

PLANNED PROFIT

PRODUCTS OR PRODUCT GROUP	ANNUAL PURCH. ($000)	TIMES ORD.-1	EST. CM MARGIN (.00)	CM. PROFIT ($000)	PLANNED PROFIT ($000)	ACTUAL MARGIN (.00)	PLAN ROII (1.X)	SALES REQ'D. ($000)	PLANNED INVENT. ($000)	TURNS REQ'D
Terminals	50	4	.20	12.50	15	.17	1.25	88.2	12.0	7.4
Monitors	35	6	.15	6.17	8	.18	1.25	44.5	6.4	7.0
CPUs	28	3	.20	7.00	10	.25	1.25	40.0	8.0	5.0
Modems	42	5	.25	1400	18	.17	1.25	82.4	11.2	7.4
Operating	25	8	.20	6.25	8	.15	1.25	16.0	1.9	8.4

Product Line Profit Analysis
ESTIMATED DISTRIBOR PROFIT

PLANNED PROFIT

PRODUCTS OR PRODUCT GROUP	ANNUAL PURCH. ($000)	TIMES ORD.-1	EST. CM MARGIN (.00)	CM. PROFIT ($000)	PLANNED PROFIT ($000)	ACTUAL MARGIN (.00)	PLAN ROII (1.X)	SALES REQ'D. ($000)	PLANNED INVENT. ($000)	TURNS REQ'D

Product Line Profit Analysis

ESTIMATED DISTRIBOR PROFIT | PLANNED PROFIT

PRODUCTS OR PRODUCT GROUP	ANNUAL PURCH. ($000)	TIMES ORD.-1	EST. CM MARGIN (.00)	CM. PROFIT ($000)	PLANNED PROFIT ($000)	ACTUAL MARGIN (.00)	PLAN ROII (1.X)	SALES REQ'D. ($000)	PLANNED INVENT. ($000)	TURNS REQ'D
Terminals	50	4	.20	12.50	15	.17	1.25	88.2	12.0	7.4
Monitors	35	6	.15	6.17	8	.18	1.25	44.5	6.4	7.0
CPUs	28	3	.20	7.00	10	.25	1.25	40.0	8.0	5.0
Modems	42	5	.25	1400	18	.17	1.25	82.4	11.2	7.4
Operating	25	8	.20	6.25	8	.15	1.25	16.0	1.9	8.4

Report of Customer Contact

DATE: _____ .

CUSTOMER NAME: _____ .

COMPANY NAME: _____ .

PHONE: _____ . FAX _____ .

REASON FOR CONTACT:

RESULTS OF DISCUSSION AND ACTION REQUIRED:

CONTACT INITIATED BY:

Report of Customer Contact

DATE: _____ .

CUSTOMER NAME: _____ .

COMPANY NAME: _____ .

PHONE: _____ . FAX _____ .

REASON FOR CONTACT:

RESULTS OF DISCUSSION AND ACTION REQUIRED:

CONTACT INITIATED BY:

Report of Customer Contact

DATE: _____ .

CUSTOMER NAME: _____ .

COMPANY NAME: _____ .

PHONE: _____ . FAX _____ .

REASON FOR CONTACT:

RESULTS OF DISCUSSION AND ACTION REQUIRED:

CONTACT INITIATED BY:

Pipeline Costs

	Days	Costs As % Of Sales Revenue
MANUFACTURING CYCLE TIME		
Procurement		
Processing		
Delivery		
DISTRIBUTOR HANDLING TIME		
Receiving		
Warehousing		
Order processing		
Delivery		
CUSTOMER REQUIREMENTS		
Receiving		
Days, inventory required		
DISTRIBUTOR INVENTORY REQUIRED		
MANUFACTURER'S INVENTORY REQUIRED		
RECEIVABLES OUTSTANDING		
ANNUAL COST of POSSESSION		
TOTAL PIPELINE COSTS		

Pipeline Costs

	Days	Costs As % Of Sales Revenue
MANUFACTURING CYCLE TIME		
Procurement	—	——
Processing	—	——
Delivery	—	——
DISTRIBUTOR HANDLING TIME		
Receiving	—	——
Warehousing	—	——
Order processing	—	——
Delivery	—	——
CUSTOMER REQUIREMENTS		
Receiving	—	——
Days, inventory required	—	——
DISTRIBUTOR INVENTORY REQUIRED	—	——
MANUFACTURER'S INVENTORY REQUIRED	—	
RECEIVABLES OUTSTANDING	—	——
ANNUAL COST of POSSESSION	——	——
TOTAL PIPELINE COSTS		——

Pipeline Costs

	Days	Costs As % Of Sales Revenue
MANUFACTURING CYCLE TIME		
Procurement		
Processing		
Delivery		
DISTRIBUTOR HANDLING TIME		
Receiving		
Warehousing		
Order processing		
Delivery		
CUSTOMER REQUIREMENTS		
Receiving		
Days, inventory required		
DISTRIBUTOR INVENTORY REQUIRED		
MANUFACTURER'S INVENTORY REQUIRED		
RECEIVABLES OUTSTANDING		
ANNUAL COST of POSSESSION		
TOTAL PIPELINE COSTS		

Workload Analysis Spreadsheet

Company Forecast $_____ 10,000,000

Distributor Name	Distributor Sales Forecast	Distributor % of Forecast	Distributor Sales	Distributor Sales/1% of Sales Forecast
_____	_____	_____	_____	_____
_____	_____	_____	_____	_____
_____	_____	_____	_____	_____
_____	_____	_____	_____	_____
_____	_____			_____
_____	_____	_____	_____	_____
_____	_____	_____	_____	_____
_____	_____	_____	_____	_____
_____	_____	_____	_____	_____
	_____		_____	_____
TOTAL				
AVERAGE	_____	_____	_____	_____

Workload Analysis Spreadsheet

Company Forecast $_____ 10,000,000

Distributor Name	Distributor Sales Forecast	Distributor % of Forecast	Distributor Sales	Distributor Sales/1% of Sales Forecast
_____	_____	_____	_____	_____
_____	_____	_____	_____	_____
_____	_____	_____	_____	_____
_____	_____	_____	_____	_____
_____	_____	_____	_____	_____
_____				_____
_____	_____	_____	_____	_____
_____	_____	_____	_____	_____
_____	_____	_____	_____	_____
_____	_____	_____	_____	_____
_____	_____	_____	_____	_____
TOTAL	_____		_____	_____
AVERAGE	_____		_____	

Workload Analysis Spreadsheet

Company Forecast $_____   10,000,000

Distributor Name	Distributor Sales Forecast	Distributor % of Forecast	Distributor Sales	Distributor Sales/1% of Sales Forecast
_____	_____	_____	_____	_____
_____	_____	_____	_____	_____
_____	_____	_____	_____	_____
_____	_____	_____	_____	_____
_____				_____
_____	_____	_____	_____	_____
_____	_____	_____	_____	_____
_____	_____	_____	_____	_____
_____	_____	_____	_____	_____
_____	_____	_____	_____	_____
TOTAL	_____	_____	_____	
AVERAGE				

Profit Rebate Table

Month	1	2	3	4	5	6	7	8	9	10	11	12
SALES FORECAST (cum.)												
ACTUAL SALES (cum.)												
MINIMUM ACCEPTABLE CONTRIBUTION MARGIN %												
PROFIT PLAN												
ACTUAL PROFIT												
REDISTRIBUTION PROFIT												

Profit Rebate Table

Month	1	2	3	4	5	6	7	8	9	10	11	12
SALES FORECAST (cum.)												
ACTUAL SALES (cum.)												
MINIMUM ACCEPTABLE CONTRIBUTION MARGIN %												
PROFIT PLAN												
ACTUAL PROFIT												
REDISTRIBUTION PROFIT												

Profit Rebate Table

Month	1	2	3	4	5	6	7	8	9	10	11	12
SALES FORECAST (cum.)												
ACTUAL SALES (cum.)												
MINIMUM ACCEPTABLE CONTRIBUTION MARGIN %												
PROFIT PLAN												
ACTUAL PROFIT												
REDISTRIBUTION PROFIT												

Report Card

KEY:

Distributor Priority / Company Rating

< PRIORITY/RATING >

Discussion Item:	5	4	3	2	1	TOTAL
Quality of Part 15674						
Competition from XYZ Co.						
Packaging of Parts						
Technical Manual Update						

Report Card

KEY:

Distributor Priority/	
	Company Rating

< PRIORITY/RATING >

Discussion Item:	5	4	3	2	1	TOTAL
Quality of Part 15674						
Competition from XYZ Co.						
Packaging of Parts						
Technical Manual Update						

Report Card

KEY:

Distributor Priority/ Company Rating	

< PRIORITY/RATING >

Discussion Item:	5	4	3	2	1	TOTAL
Quality of Part 15674						
Competition from XYZ Co.						
Packaging of Parts						
Technical Manual Update						

Index